New Junior Cycle
English Higher Lev

GW00359793

Contents

Student Study Essentials

Completed
(✓)

Please note: There was no exam in 2021 and 2020 for English Higher Level.

FREE ONLINE SOLUTIONS
**Visit www.e-xamit.ie to access Free Online Tutorials
with Sample Answers, Hints and Tips! (See codes inside.)**

Photographs in Edco sample papers: Alamy p203, p214, p271, p284; RSC p227; all other photos Shutterstock.com

Welcome to Junior Cycle English Studies
Guide to Better Grades

Higher Level

Marks: 180

Time allowed: 2 hours

For your Junior Cycle English course, you will sit a two-hour examination at the end of third year. The examination will be linked to what you have learned in second and third year and to the learning outcomes for final assessment (see page vi). In any given year, a selection of learning outcomes will be assessed.

There will be no set sections and no set number of questions.

Stimulus Material

You will be given some stimulus material (for example, a poem, an extract from a play or novel, a poster, the text of a talk, a screen shot from a website) and asked to complete some tasks.

Typically, these tasks will involve:

- Comprehending – reading for information; following an argument; summarising ideas; linking to other ideas; questioning and evaluating ideas.
- Reading to appreciate – reading and identifying the various ways writers and speakers enrich their language and engage their audience; identifying how writers and speakers use language for different purposes.
- Responding – a variety of creative or functional writing tasks arising from the stimulus material.

Responding to Studied Texts

As well as questions on the stimulus material you could be asked to write about the texts you studied for your English course. You will be expected to write in a way that shows you have the language to write about poems, novels, plays, films and multi-modal texts. You will use this language to show your appreciation of such things as: characters, setting, themes, story and action; as well as identifying and discussing key scenes and favourite images.

Writing for a Variety of Purposes

At different points on the examination paper, you could be asked to write in a particular form (for example, letter, diary, blog, review, story) for a given purpose. In fact, there could be a whole section given over to writing.

General Advice

Because there is no set format for the paper, YOU MUST READ ALL THE INSTRUCTIONS VERY CAREFULLY.

Look carefully at the marks allocated to each section and then to individual questions.

This rough guide will help you plan your time.

Do not spend more time on a question than it is worth.

5-mark question	3 minutes
10-mark question	6 minutes
15-mark question	10 minutes
20-mark question	12 minutes
25-mark question	15 minutes
30-mark question	20 minutes
40-mark question	25 minutes
50-mark question	30 minutes
60-mark question/section	40 minutes
70-mark question/section	45 minutes
80-mark question/section	50 minutes
90-mark question/section	55 minutes
100-mark question/section	60 minutes

Exam Hints and Tips

Advice on Reading

Always read a text twice before you begin to answer questions. To help you complete the tasks, keep in mind the intended audience for the text and the purpose for which it was written.

Read the instructions carefully. If a question asks for your opinion, make sure you explain your point-of-view and, if you can, find evidence in the passage to support it.

If you are asked a question and you are not sure about the answer, try to find clues in the text to help you.

Remember that handwriting, spelling and expression are important, so be as neat and as accurate as you can.

Advice on Writing

Read the question and the instructions carefully. These will determine what style of writing is appropriate to the task. No matter what the purpose of your writing, do some rough work. This will enable you to try out ideas and make a plan. You should make sure that the tone, style and language of your writing matches the purpose and the form. A letter to your school principal will be more formal than an email to your best friend.

Writing tasks give you an opportunity to show that you can write intelligently, fluently and with a clear sense of purpose, control and enjoyment.

Neat handwriting, correct spelling and punctuation and the use of paragraphs will enhance the experience of your reader.

Advice on Writing about Studied Texts

If you are asked to write about a text you have studied, be sure that you know the title of the text and the name of the author or, in the case of a film, the director.

For narrative texts, you need to know the story, and be familiar with the characters and their relationships. You also need to have some ideas on the writer's skill in telling the story, how they enrich the language of the text and how they engage their readers.

For poetry, make a list of topics and themes dealt with in the poems you have studied. Apart from knowing what a poem is about, you need to study the language of the poem and the techniques used by the poet to bring the poem to life, including such things as imagery and sound.

In writing about the texts you have studied, show the examiner that you have read the texts carefully and thought about them. Express your thoughts in a clear style, and present your ideas in a logical manner.

And finally

An examination is an opportunity for you to show what you can do and to share your love for English and the texts you have read. Write with energy and conviction! Be clear! Be confident!

Note on Assessment Task Arrangements 2023/2024

No Assessment Tasks are required for third year Junior Cycle students for the academic year 2023/2024:

'As a result of the decision to extend adjustments made to assessment arrangements for the 2022/2023 academic year to the 2023/2024 academic year, the requirement to complete Assessment Tasks has been removed for third year Junior Cycle students in the 2023/2024 academic year.' – NCCA

Tick each paper as you complete it and tick the sections on each paper.

Record the marks allocated per section and the recommended time.

Junior Cycle English HL	Marks	Time	2023	2022	2019	2018	2017	SEC Sample 2	SEC Sample 3	Edco Sample A	Edco Sample B	Edco Sample C	Edco Sample D	Edco Sample E
Appreciating Audience														
Reading to Appreciate														
Reading to Understand														
Reading Comprehension														
Responding to Studied Texts														
Responding Imaginatively														
Writing for a Variety of Purposes														
Exam Complete														

Junior Cycle English Studies
Grading of the Final Examination

Grade Range	%
Distinction	90 to 100
Higher Merit	75 but less than 90
Merit	55 but less than 75
Achieved	40 but less than 55
Partially Achieved	20 but less than 40
Not Graded	0 but less than 20

Source: State Examinations Commission, 2023.

Study Hub

Your free online guide to smarter study.

Visit

www.edco.ie/onlinestudyhub

Remember

- You must answer all sections.
- Pay attention to the marks allocated to each section.
- Plan your time.
- Read instructions carefully

Map Your Progress!

New Junior Cycle Learning Outcomes Explained

These are the learning outcomes upon which the final assessment will be based.

Strand: Oral Language

Engaging with oral language – students should be able to:

- Listen actively in order to interpret meaning, compare, evaluate effectiveness of, and respond to drama, poetry, media broadcasts, digital media, noting key ideas, style, tone, content and overall impact in a systematic way
- Demonstrate how register (language style), including grammar, text structure and word choice, varies with context and purpose in spoken texts

Strand: Reading

Engaging in reading – students should be able to:

- Read texts with fluency, understanding and competence, decoding groups of words/phrases and not just single words
- Read for a variety of purposes: learning, pleasure, research, comparison
- Use a wide range of reading comprehension strategies appropriate to texts, including digital texts: to retrieve information; to link to previous knowledge, follow a process or argument, summarise, link main ideas; to monitor their own understanding; to question, analyse, synthesise and evaluate
- Use an appropriate critical vocabulary while responding to literary texts
- Read their texts for understanding and appreciation of character, setting, story and action: to explore how and why characters develop, and to recognise the importance of setting and plot structure
- Select key moments from their texts and give thoughtful value judgements on the main character, a key scene, a favourite image from a film, a poem, a drama, a chapter, a media- or web-based event
- Read their texts to understand and appreciate language enrichment by examining an author's choice of words, the use and effect of simple figurative language, vocabulary and language patterns, and images, as appropriate to the text
- Identify, appreciate and compare the ways in which different literary, digital and visual genres and sub-genres shape texts and shape the reader's experience of them
- Identify and comment on features of English at word and sentence level using appropriate terminology, showing how such features contribute to overall effect
- Understand how word choice, syntax, grammar and text structure may vary with context and purpose
- Appreciate a variety of registers (language style) and understand their use in the written context

Strand: Writing

Engaging in reading – students should be able to:

- Demonstrate their understanding that there is a clear purpose for all writing activities and be able to plan, draft, re-draft and edit their own writing as appropriate
- Write for a variety of purposes, for example to analyse, evaluate, imagine, explore, engage, amuse, narrate, inform, explain, argue, persuade, criticise, comment on what they have heard, viewed and read
- Write competently in a range of text forms, for example letter, report, multi-modal text, review, blog, using appropriate vocabulary, tone and a variety of styles to achieve a chosen purpose for different audiences
- Use editing skills continuously during the writing process to enhance meaning and impact: select vocabulary, reorder words, phrases and clauses, correct punctuation and spelling, reorder paragraphs, remodel, manage content
- Respond imaginatively in writing to their texts showing a critical appreciation of language, style and content, choice of words, language patterns, tone, images
- Write about the effectiveness of key moments from their texts commenting on characters, key scenes, favourite images from a film, a poem, a drama, a chapter, a media- or web-based event
- Engage in the writing process as a private, pleasurable and purposeful activity and using a personal voice as their individual style is thoughtfully developed over the years
- Use and apply their knowledge of language structures, for example sentence structure, paragraphing, grammar, to make their writing a richer experience for themselves and the reader
- Use language conventions appropriately, especially punctuation and spelling, to aid meaning and presentation and to enhance the reader's experience
- Demonstrate an understanding of how syntax, grammar, text structure and word choice may vary with context and purpose

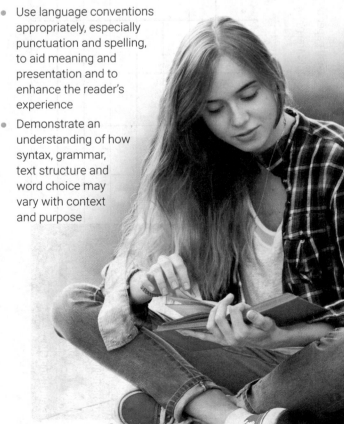

2023

Coimisiún na Scrúduithe Stáit
State Examinations Commission

Junior Cycle Final Examination 2023

English

Higher Level

Wednesday 7 June   Morning 9:30 – 11:30

180 marks

Examination Number

Day and Month of Birth

For example, 3rd February is
entered as 0302

Centre Stamp

The theme of this examination paper is
The Art of Storytelling

Instructions

There are **four** sections in this paper.

Section A	Understanding Characters and Film	40 marks	2 questions
Section B	Narrative in Poetry	50 marks	3 questions
Section C	Appreciating Story	55 marks	2 questions
Section D	Shaping Stories and Emotions	35 marks	3 questions

Answer **all** 10 questions.

The questions do not all carry equal marks. The number of marks for each question is stated at the top of the question.

You should spend about 25 minutes on Section A, 30 minutes on Section B, 35 minutes on Section C and 25 minutes on Section D.

When answering on studied material, you must use texts in line with what is prescribed for this year.

Write your answers in the spaces provided in this booklet. You may lose marks if you do not do so. You are not required to use all of the space provided. You should read each question in full before beginning your response.

Extra pages are provided if needed. Label any extra work clearly with the question number and part.

You may only use blue or black pen when writing your answers. Do not use pencil.

This examination booklet will be scanned and your work will be presented to an examiner on screen. Anything that you write outside of the answer areas may not be seen by the examiner.

Where used in a question on film, the term 'character' is understood to refer to both real people and fictional characters.

| **Section A** | **Understanding Characters and Film** | **40 marks** |

Suggested time for Section A: 25 minutes

Read the following five writing tips for creating characters in stories. These tips were inspired by tweets written by a Pixar screenwriter for film. Pixar movies appeal to audiences of all ages. Answer the questions that follow.

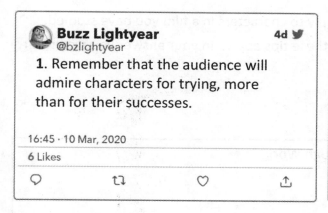

Buzz Lightyear @bzlightyear — 4d

1. Remember that the audience will admire characters for trying, more than for their successes.

16:45 · 10 Mar, 2020
6 Likes

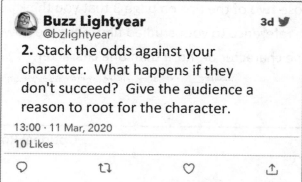

Buzz Lightyear @bzlightyear — 3d

2. Stack the odds against your character. What happens if they don't succeed? Give the audience a reason to root for the character.

13:00 · 11 Mar, 2020
10 Likes

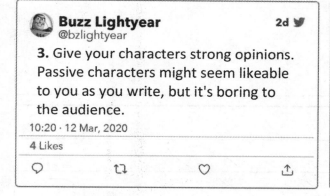

Buzz Lightyear @bzlightyear — 2d

3. Give your characters strong opinions. Passive characters might seem likeable to you as you write, but it's boring to the audience.

10:20 · 12 Mar, 2020
4 Likes

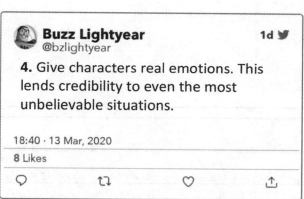

Buzz Lightyear @bzlightyear — 1d

4. Give characters real emotions. This lends credibility to even the most unbelievable situations.

18:40 · 13 Mar, 2020
8 Likes

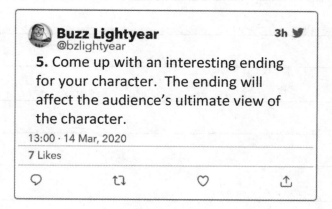

Buzz Lightyear @bzlightyear — 3h

5. Come up with an interesting ending for your character. The ending will affect the audience's ultimate view of the character.

13:00 · 14 Mar, 2020
7 Likes

Question 1   (20 marks)

Choose a film you have studied.

Title of film:	Spider-man
Director:	Sam Raimi.

Choose **two** of the tips on page 3 that you think apply to characters in a film you have studied.
With reference to your studied film, describe how these tips apply. In your answer you may refer
to one character or more than one character.

Optional Rough Work

Although the movie came out nearly twenty-two
years ago it still holds a special place in my
heart and the hearts of millions of people in
the world and does an excellent job demonstrating
all five of the tips on page 3. Peter Parker
the protagonist of the film starts off as a
regular teenager untill he is bitten by a radioactive
spider. He soon then discovers he has gained
super human abilities, alongside this Peter has
a love intrest Mary Jane Whatson who he spends th

Film trying to win her over while also adapting to his new powers and Spider-man persona, this gives him 1 in goal 1, 2, Real emotion. During the movie we also find out that Peters bestfriends dad is the antagonist who has been terrorizing the city and the film culminates with the antagonist accidentally killing himself giving the story an interesting ending.

Question 2 (20 marks)

Film directors often create key moments through the use of striking visual images. With reference to one or more key moment(s) from the film you have studied, explain how the director's use of striking visual images makes your chosen moment(s) engaging for the viewer.

themes

characters

characters

Characters

understanding of the themes better

Optional Rough Work

[handwritten text, largely illegible:]

Throughout the film the director used themes

gives close ups... the characters... as

most... of... show the emotions

of the characters... accurately

Additional writing space. Label all work clearly with the question number and part.

Suggested time for Section B: 30 minutes

phgtgg
Visit www.e-xamit.ie

Read the following poem and answer the questions that follow.

An Apology

Sincere apologies, too late I know, for not getting engaged
on the night we'd planned, Christmas Eve 1962. I had the ring
in my pocket, the one we'd bought together that November
from the little jewellers on Whitefriargate in Hull. Remember?

After Midnight Mass, arm-in-arming back to ours,
we linger outside the gates of Seaforth Park. The moon
smiling and expectant. No wind, no people, no cars.
Sheets of ice are nailed to the streets with stars.

The scene is set, two lovers on the silver screen.
A pause, the copy-book kiss. Did angels sing?
This was my moment, the cue to pledge my troth*,
to take out the blue, velvet box, and do my stuff.

But marriage was a bridge I feared might be detonated,
And I had this crazy idea that if I didn't mention it, then you
wouldn't either. That we'd collude in romantic amnesia.
That life would go on as before. What could be easier?

Christmas passed. Enraged, you blew up. I felt the blast.
We got engaged. It didn't last.

Roger McGough

* Promise to marry/propose

Question 3   **(10 marks)**

In this narrative poem we hear the story from the man's perspective. Tell the story from the woman's perspective. Write in the first person.

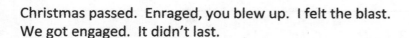

Optional Rough Work

(blank lined answer space)

Question 4 (15 marks)

Roger McGough uses vivid imagery in this poem. Identify the two images that appealed to you the most. Explain your choices with reference to the poem.

Optional Rough Work

Question 5   **(25 marks)**

Read all parts of this question carefully before writing your answers in the appropriate spaces below.

You may not use the poem printed on this paper when answering this question.

Narrative poems often tell interesting personal stories.

Choose a poem you have studied that tells a personal story.

| Title of poem: |
| Name of poet: |

(a) Outline what happens in your chosen poem and explain what the poem reveals to you about people. Support your response using suitable quotation from the poem.

(b) In your view, does the poet use imagery effectively to tell the personal story? Explain your answer using suitable quotation from the poem.

Answer space for part **(a)**

Optional Rough Work

Answer space for part **(b)**

Optional Rough Work

Additional writing space. Label all work clearly with the question number and part.

Suggested time for Section C: 35 minutes

Read the following extract from Shakespeare's play, *Hamlet*. The old king, Hamlet's father, has died and has been replaced by Claudius, Hamlet's uncle. In this scene, the ghost of the old king tells Hamlet the story of how he died. Answer the questions that follow.

Ghost: I am thy father's spirit,
Doomed for a certain term to walk the night...
I am forbid
To tell the secrets of my prison house,
I could a tale unfold whose lightest word
Would harrow up thy soul, freeze thy young blood,
Make thy two eyes, like stars, start from their spheres,
Thy knotted and combined locks to part
And each particular hair to stand on end...
But this eternal blazon must not be   10
To ears of flesh and blood. List, List, O, listen!
If thou didst ever thy dear father love –

Hamlet: O God!

Ghost: Revenge his foul and most unnatural murder.

Hamlet: Murder?

Ghost: Murder most foul, as in the best it is.
But this most foul, strange and unnatural.

Hamlet: Haste me to know't, that I, with wings as swift
As meditation or the thoughts of love,
May sweep to my revenge.   20

Ghost: I find thee apt...
Now, Hamlet, hear.
'Tis given out that, sleeping in my orchard,
A serpent stung me. So the whole ear of Denmark
Is by a forged process of my death
Rankly abused. But know, thou noble youth,
The serpent that did sting thy father's life
Now wears his crown.

Hamlet: O my prophetic soul! My uncle?

Question 6   **(20 marks)**

In the case of parts (a) to (c), indicate the correct answer by placing a tick ✓ in the appropriate box. Tick **one** box only in each case.

(a)   If Hamlet's father was to describe the world he now inhabits, how would Hamlet react?

Hamlet would be horrified.   ☐

Hamlet would be comforted.   ☐

Hamlet would want to join him.   ☐

(b)   According to the following lines what does Hamlet intend to do:

> *Haste me to know't, that I, with wings as swift*
> *As meditation or the thoughts of love,*
> *May sweep to my revenge.* (Lines 18 – 20)?

He will take action speedily.   ☐

He will think about his next move very carefully.   ☐

He will get away from this ghost as quickly as possible.   ☐

(c)   Which one of the following is the best explanation of the lines:

> *So the whole ear of Denmark*
> *Is by a forged process of my death*
> *Rankly abused.* (Lines 24 – 26)?

Hamlet's father's death is a hot topic of conversation in Denmark.   ☐

The people of Denmark are outraged by Hamlet's father's death.   ☐

The people of Denmark have been lied to about how Hamlet's father died.   ☐

(d)   Explain what you think Hamlet means when he says: 'O my prophetic soul! My uncle?' at the end of the extract.

<table>
<tr><td></td></tr>
<tr><td></td></tr>
<tr><td></td></tr>
<tr><td></td></tr>
<tr><td></td></tr>
</table>

(e) Portraying ghosts on stage is challenging for theatre directors. Describe **one** way a ghost could be represented effectively on stage for a modern audience.

```
_____
_____
_____
_____
_____
_____
_____
_____
```

Question 7   (35 marks)

Following your study of English for Junior Cycle, you have been asked to give a talk to a group of young readers about:

The Art of Good Storytelling.

Write the text of the talk you would deliver, discussing at least three aspects of the art of good storytelling in either the prescribed Shakespearean play **or** one of the novels that you have studied.

Optional Rough Work

Title of text used:

Additional writing space. Label all work clearly with the question number and part.

Suggested time for Section D: 25 minutes

Question 8 (10 marks)

All well-written stories have a shape or structure. One popular shape for a story is called the *Man in Hole* shape. Study the graphic image below which illustrates the three steps that a typical *Man in Hole* story takes. Complete the task that follows.

© Maya Eilam

Starting with Step 1 below, outline a plot summary for a story using the three steps presented in the *Man in Hole* graphic above.

Optional Rough Work

Step 1: It was an ordinary day for Alex until...
Step 2:
Step 3:

Question 9 (5 marks)

Rewrite the following text, adding capital letters, commas, inverted commas, apostrophes and full stops correctly. You should create three lines of direct speech.

tell me a story jane implored youre too old for stories her father sighed ill never be too old for stories jane insisted

Question 10   **(20 marks)**

Choose either picture **A** or picture **B** below. Imagine that your chosen picture shows a character in a short story you are writing. Write the opening paragraph for that story in which you make this character either a villain or a hero. You may include dialogue in your paragraph.

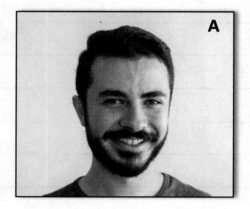 

Optional Rough Work

Chosen character:

Additional writing space. Label all work clearly with the question number and part.

Additional writing space. Label all work clearly with the question number and part.

Additional writing space. Label all work clearly with the question number and part

Acknowledgements

Images
Images on page 3: https://www.iposters.co.uk/toy-story-buzz-lightyear-124955
Image on page 9: © Jeremy Bishop on Unsplash
Image on page 12 : shutterstock.com
Image on page 16: Alamy
Image on page 22: Man in Hole infographic © Maya Eilam
Images on page 24: shutterstock.com; stayglam.com

Texts
Acuna, Kirsten. 22 Storytelling Tips For Writers From A Pixar Storyboard Artist: businessinsider.com
Shakespeare, William. Hamlet, Arden. London: Bloomsbury, 2016
McGough, Roger. An Apology. Holiday on Death Row. London: Cape, 1979. Printed by permission of
United Agents (www.unitedagents.co.uk) on behalf of Roger McGough.

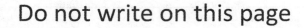

Do not write on this page

Junior Cycle Final Examination – Higher Level

English

Wednesday 7 June

Morning 9:30 – 11:30

2023J002A1EL2828

Coimisiún na Scrúduithe Stáit
State Examinations Commission

Junior Cycle Final Examination 2022

English

Higher Level

Wednesday 8 June   Morning 9:30 – 11:30

180 marks

Examination Number

Day and Month of Birth

For example, 3rd February is
entered as 0302

Centre Stamp

The theme of this examination paper is
Hope

Instructions

There are **four** sections in this examination paper.

Section A	Writing to Engage with your Audience	40 marks	3 questions
Section B	Appreciating Figurative Language	70 marks	3 questions
Section C	Reading Images in Film	30 marks	2 questions
Section D	Responding to Texts	40 marks	2 questions

Answer all 10 questions.

The questions do not all carry equal marks. The number of marks for each question is stated at the top of the question.

You should spend about 25 minutes on Section A, 45 minutes on Section B, 20 minutes on Section C and 25 minutes on Section D.

When answering on studied material, you must use texts in line with what is prescribed for 2022.

Write your answers in the spaces provided in this booklet. You may lose marks if you do not do so. You are not required to use all of the space provided. You should read each question in full before beginning your response.

Extra pages are provided if needed. Label any extra work clearly with the question number and part.

You may only use blue or black pen when writing your answers. Do not use pencil.

This examination booklet will be scanned and your work will be presented to an examiner on screen. Anything that you write outside of the answer areas may not be seen by the examiner.

Suggested time for Section A: 25 minutes

Study the quotation below. It is a quotation by Dr. Seuss that is commonly used by speakers in school graduation ceremonies.

Oh, the Places You'll Go!

You'll be on your way up!
You'll be seeing great sights!
You'll join the high fliers
Who soar to high heights

You're off to Great Places,
Today is your day!
Your mountain is waiting.
So… *get on your way!*

Question 1   **(10 marks)**

Do you think the Dr. Seuss quotation above is a suitable choice for graduation ceremonies? Explain your answer.

Optional Rough Work

31

I think the Dr. Seuss quotation is very suitable for a graduation ceremony because the quote is all about "soaring to new heights" ~~indicating~~ which is very fitting for a graduation as when you graduate you now have opened new doors of possibility so "today is your day" is perfect as now that you have graduated there are endless possibilities for what you can do with your life.

Question 2 (25 marks)

You are writing your diary at the end of a very eventful day.

23rd January. Dear Diary,
You won't believe what has happened! Today has been a day that filled me with hope...

Continue the diary entry below. Write in the first person.

2022

23 January. Dear Diary,

You won't believe what has happened! Today has been a day that filled me with hope...

Question 3 **(5 marks)**

Rewrite each one of the sentences in the space below it, correcting **one** error in each case.

(a) I cannot except that it is a hopeless situation.

accept

(b) Where did I leave my lucky hat.

(c) There is alot of optimism in the school at present.

(d) "Your always so cheerful," Sophie said.

(e) There is some people who always look on the bright side of things.

Additional Writing Space. Label all work clearly with the question number and part.

Suggested time for Section B: 45 minutes

Read the following poem by Ada Limón and answer the questions that follow.

Instructions on Not Giving Up

More than the fuchsia funnels breaking out
of the crabapple tree, more than the neighbour's
almost obscene display of cherry limbs shoving
their cotton candy-coloured blossoms to the slate
sky of Spring rains, it's the greening of the trees
that really gets to me. When all the shock of white
and taffy*, the world's baubles and trinkets, leave
the pavement strewn with the confetti of aftermath,
the leaves come. Patient, plodding, a green skin
growing over whatever winter did to us, a return
to the strange idea of continuous living despite
the mess of us, the hurt, the empty. Fine then,
I'll take it, the tree seems to say, a new slick leaf
unfurling like a fist to an open palm. I'll take it all.

Fuchsia flowers

* A colourful sweet

Question 4   **(25 marks)**

(a) 'it's the greening of the trees that really gets to me.' Do you think that this is a positive or a negative statement by the poet? Explain your answer with reference to the poem.

Optional Rough Work

(b) Would you recommend this poem for inclusion in a poetry book for Junior Cycle English? In your answer you should refer to both what the poem says and how it uses language.

Optional Rough Work

Question 5   **(10 marks)**

Give an example of a memorable metaphor or simile used by a poet that you encountered in your
study of English for Junior Cycle. Explain why this metaphor or simile was memorable for you.
You may not use the poem printed on this paper.

Optional Rough Work

Question 6   **(35 marks)**

Do you think that poets offer readers hope through their poetry? Explain your views with
reference to at least three poems you have studied. Refer to both the ideas and the use of
language in the poems you discuss. You may not use the poem printed on this paper but you may
use the poem you referred to in question 5.

Optional Rough Work

Poem titles:

Answer:

Additional writing space. Label all work clearly with the question number and part.

Suggested time for Section C: 20 minutes

Question 7 (10 marks)

Study the following poster about camera shots in film and match each definition to the appropriate film image on page 17 by inserting the correct number in the table below.

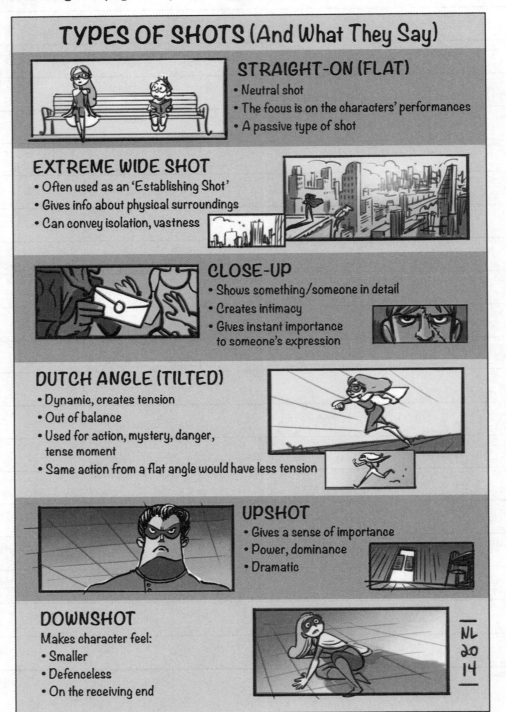

Camera Shot	Number
Straight-On	5
Extreme Wide shot	3
Close Up	1
Dutch	4
Upshot	6
Downshot	2

Question 8   **(20 marks)**

Imagine you are the director of the film you have studied. Discuss how at least two of the types of shots identified in the poster on page 16 could have been used in key moments in the film to enhance the viewing experience for the audience. The actual director may or may not have used these shots in the film.

Optional Rough Work

Title of film:	
Name of director:	

Additional Writing Space. Label all work clearly with the question number and part.

Suggested time for Section D: 25 minutes

Read the following passage which is the ending to a novel by Douglas Coupland. Answer the question that follows. Sarah, an astronaut who has a physical disability, is going on a space mission. In the passage she is parting company with her mother Janet and brother Wade before her voyage.

As the chopper pulled into NASA, Sarah remembered something and mentioned it to Janet and Wade: 'Guys, I'm allowed to bring twelve ounces of personal belongings up into space with me. Do either of you have a lightweight object you'd like to be able to show-and-tell in ten years' time and say, *This was once up in space!*'

Wade and Janet looked at each other, then Wade removed a letter from his shirt pocket, before he handed it to Sarah, he asked her, 'Sarah, are you going on a spacewalk on this trip?'

    'Outside the craft?'

    'Yeah.'

    'Yes I am.'

    'So if you were to leave something out there, that would circle the planet for ever?'

    'For a pretty long time.'

    'Take this for me.' He gave her the letter. 'But don't bring it back, OK? Leave it out there, out in orbit.'

Sarah looked at the letter and made no historical connection. 'Sure.'

    'You promise?'

Sarah wondered what he was up to. 'I promise.'

    'Good.' Wade made a face that might have been made by pioneers crossing the continent, dropping a piano off their overloaded wagon onto the wheezy Oklahoma dirt – a burden relieved.

    'What about you, Mom?'

    'Could you pass me a pair of those scissors there, dear?'

    'Scissors? What for?'

    'Please, I need them just for a second.'

Sarah handed them to Janet, who reached back, pulled her hair into a ponytail and quickly snipped off the large lock.

    'There.'

    'Mom!'

    'Oh shush girl. And these are excellent scissors. I'd like to get a pair for myself.'

    'Mom, why did you – '

Janet quickly tied the severed ponytail into a neat knot.

'Mom, you're scaring me.'

'Sarah, answer me this – if you were to be out in space, and if you threw an object down to Earth, it would burn through the atmosphere on re-entry, wouldn't it?'

'What – throw it down to Earth?'

'Yes, dear.'

'But why?'

'Because people will look up to its trail when it falls down. They won't know it, but it will be *me* they're looking at.'

'And – ?'

'And they'll think they've just seen a star.'

Question 9   (15 marks)

To what extent do you think the author of this passage succeeds in writing an ending with a sense of hope? Support your answer with reference to the passage.

Optional Rough Work

_____

_____

_____

_____

_____

_____

_____

_____

_____

_____

_____

_____

_____

_____

_____

Question 10 (25 marks)

Whether it is a book we have read or a play we have seen, good texts can have a long-lasting effect on the thoughts and feelings of the reader or viewer.

With reference to at least two key moments from **either** a novel or a play you have studied, explain how the novel or play had a long-lasting effect on your thoughts and feelings.

Title of novel or play:
Name of writer:

Optional Rough Work

Additional Writing Space. Label all work clearly with the question number and part.

Additional Writing Space. Label all work clearly with the question number and part.

Acknowledgements

Images
Image on page 31: https://theconversation.com
Image on page 32: https://www.dailymailgh.com/episode-7-when-the-sun-pointed-south/
Image on page 36: https://www.nature-and-garden.com/gardening/fuschia.html
Image on page 39: https://www.goodreads.com/author_blog_posts/16904310-symbol-metaphor-and-simile----oh-my
Image on page 40: https://theconversation.com/how-hope-can-keep-you-healthier-and-happier-132507
Image on page 44: https:rizandnorm.tumblr.com/post/87036475303/tuesday-tips-types-of-shots-and-what-they-say
Images on page 45: https://www.premiumbeat.com/blog/how-to-shoot-close-up-shots-like-sergio-leone/;
https://nofilmschool.com/high-angle-shot-definition-examples; https://nofilmschool.com/high-angle-shot-definition-examples; https://images2.fanpop.com/images/photos/4100000/Forrest-Gump-forrest-gump-4161288-1014-419.jpg;
https://videomaker.com
Image on page 46: https://newdawnfilm.com/overcoming-the-fear-of-being-a-filmmaker/
Image on page 49: https://www.dkfindout.com/uk/space/life-in-space/spacewalk/
Images on page 51: https://www.familyeducation.com/young-adult-books/20-books-for-teens-to-read-before-they-turn-18; https://lithub.com/teaching-students-to-use-their-voices-through-theater/

Texts
Dr. Seuss. "Oh, the Places You'll Go!", www.goodreads.com
Limón, Ada. "Instructions on Not Giving Up", www.poets.org
Coupland, Douglas. *All Families are Psychotic,* Random House of Canada

Material may have been adapted, for the purpose of assessment, without the authors' prior consent.

2022

Junior Cycle Final Examination – Higher Level

English

Wednesday 8 June

Morning 9:30 – 11:30

2022J002A1EL2828

Coimisiún na Scrúduithe Stáit

State Examinations Commission

Junior Cycle Final Examination 2019

English

Higher Level

Wednesday 5 June – Morning 9:30 – 11:30

180 marks

Examination number				

Centre Stamp

Instructions

There are **four** sections in this examination paper.

Section A	Showing Critical Appreciation	50 marks	4 questions
Section B	Reading and Responding to Texts	50 marks	3 questions
Section C	Giving Thoughtful Value Judgements	40 marks	1 question
Section D	Using a Personal Voice	40 marks	2 questions

Answer all 10 questions.

The questions do not all carry equal marks. The number of marks for each question is stated at the top of the question.

You should spend about 35 minutes on Section A, 40 minutes on Section B, 20 minutes on Section C and 20 minutes on Section D.

When answering on studied material, you must use texts in line with what is prescribed for 2019.

Write your answers in the spaces provided in this booklet. You may lose marks if you do not do so. You are not required to use all of the space provided. You should read each question in full before beginning your response.

Extra pages are provided if needed. Label any extra work clearly with the question number and part.

You may only use blue or black pen when writing your answers. Do not use pencil.

This examination booklet will be scanned and your work will be presented to an examiner on screen. Anything that you write outside of the answer areas may not be seen by the examiner.

Suggested time for Section A: 35 minutes

Read the following poem by Paul Durcan and answer the questions that follow.

Caught Out

Face to face with a lamb
On a Spring evening at twilight
I have nowhere to hide

Black legs, black ears,
White baby-grow,
Two black eyes peer up at me

I feel as guilty
As if caught out by my grand-daughter
Telling her a lie.

Question 1 (10 marks)

Do you find the poet's reaction to the lamb in this poem surprising? Explain your answer with reference to the poem.

Optional Rough Work

(blank lined answer box)

Question 2   **(15 marks)**

Do you think Paul Durcan uses language effectively in his poem, 'Caught Out'? Explain your answer with reference to any **two** examples chosen from the poem.

Optional Rough Work

Question 3   **(5 marks)**

Choose from the list of poetic terms in **bold** below to complete the table, by matching the term to the **most appropriate** line of verse. The first example is completed for you. (Use each word only once.)

Alliteration   Onomatopoeia   Hyperbole   Metaphor   Assonance   Simile

A tap at the pane, the quick sharp scratch...	**Onomatopoeia**
What happens to a dream deferred? Does it dry up Like a raisin in the sun?	
The fair breeze blew, the white foam flew, The furrow followed free...	
All the world's a stage, and all the men and women merely players.	
And a river of green is sliding unseen beneath the trees...	
But I would walk 500 miles, And I would walk 500 more, Just to be the man who walks a 1,000 miles to fall down at your door.	

Question 4   **(20 marks)**

Read parts **(a)** and **(b)** carefully before writing your answers in the appropriate spaces below. You may not use the poem printed on this paper when answering this question.

(a)   *Poems often explore themes that challenge us to stop and think.*

      Select a poem you have studied and explain why a theme in this poem challenged you to stop and think. Use the poem to support your response.

(b)   Do you think the poet uses language effectively in your chosen poem? Explain your answer, supporting your response with suitable quotation from the poem.

Title of poem:

Name of poet:

Answer space for part **(a)**.

Optional Rough Work

Answer space for part (b).

Optional Rough Work

Additional Writing Space. Label all work clearly with the question number and part.

Suggested time for Section B: 40 minutes

Study the following text and answer question five. The text is an infographic that aims to convey advice about how to become more creative.

2019

xzhroj
Visit www.e-xamit.ie

Question 5 (5 marks)

State and explain **one** reason why you think the infographic is or is not effective in conveying advice about how to become more creative.

The Nobel Prize in Literature

Seamus Heaney, Nobel Prize 1995

(1) Since 1901, the Nobel Prizes have been honouring men and women from all corners of the globe for their outstanding achievements. The Nobel Prizes were the brainchild of Alfred B. Nobel, a Swedish industrialist, best known in his lifetime for inventing dynamite. Having no immediate heirs, Nobel declared in his will, that part of his vast fortune should be used annually to reward people who, "have conferred the greatest benefit to mankind", in five different categories.

(2) Among the prizes provided for in Nobel's will, one was intended for literature. The annual winner is decided by the Swedish Academy in Stockholm. The Academy explains the reason for their choice each year in a citation. This citation is a statement about the qualities and merits of the winner's work.

- In 2017, novelist Kazuo Ishiguro was the winner. The Academy cited him for, *"novels of great emotional force"*.
- In 2016, the prize went to American singer / songwriter, Bob Dylan for, *"having created new poetic expressions within the great American song tradition"*.
- In 2013 the prize was awarded to Alice Munro for being a, *"master of the short story"*.
- In 1995, the winner was the poet Seamus Heaney. The citation praised his, *"works of lyrical beauty and ethical depth which exalt everyday miracles and the living past"*.
- And in 1991 the winner was writer Nadine Gordimer, *"who through her magnificent writing has... been of very great benefit to humanity"*.

Alfred Nobel regarded various forms of expression as opportunities to achieve greater understanding of our own thoughts, lives and relationships with other people and our surroundings.

Winners of the Nobel Prize in Literature are awarded the prize by the Academy for various qualities in their writings. Based on your reading of part **(2)** of the article, identify any **two** of the qualities in the winners' work, rewarded by the Academy in the past, and explain which **one** of these qualities, in your view, is more important in works of literature.

Optional Rough Work

2019

Question 6 [10 marks]

Winners of the Nobel Prize in literature are awarded the prize by the Academy for various qualities in their writings. Based on your reading of their (2) of the aforementioned any two of the qualities in the winners' work, rewarded by the Academy in the past, and explain which one of these qualities, in your view, is more important in works of literature.

Optional Rough Work

Question 7 (35 marks)

Parts **(a)** and **(b)** of this question are linked. Read both parts carefully before beginning your answer.

(a) Imagine that one of the novels you have studied has won an award called,
The Junior Cycle English, Best Read Award, 2019.

Write a short citation for the novel receiving the award. In the citation you should identify the main reason why, in your view, the novel deserves the award. (A citation is a statement about the qualities and merits of a winner's work.) (5)

Title of novel:
Author:

Optional Rough Work

Citation for the award-winning novel

(b) With reference to at least two key moments in your chosen novel, discuss why the citation you proposed in part **(a)** is justified. (30)

Optional Rough Work

Optional Rough Work

Additional Writing Space. Label all work clearly with the question number and part.

2019

Suggested time for Section C: 20 minutes

Question 8   **(40 marks)**

By creating characters that express strong views, playwrights can heighten the drama in plays.

(a)   With reference to a Shakespearean **or** a non-Shakespearean play you have studied, outline a key moment when a character expresses a strong view and explain how this heightens the drama in the play.

(b)   If you were to stage the key moment you have chosen, explain **two** things you would do in order to heighten the dramatic experience for the audience. You may refer to aspects of performance and / or stagecraft.

Title of play:

Name of playwright:

Answer space for part **(a)**.

Optional Rough Work

705

Oisín Maher

Answer space for part **(b)**.

Optional Rough Work

Additional writing space. Label all work clearly with the question number and part.

Suggested time for Section D: 20 minutes

The 'Sound Off' series of articles in *The Irish Times*, gives people an opportunity to air their own views, in their own unique way, on an issue that annoys them. Read the article below by Aoife Dooley and respond to the tasks that follow it.

txchod
Visit www.e-xamit.ie

Question 9 (15 marks)

Do you find Aoife Dooley's article entertaining? Explain your answer with reference to the text. You may refer to the article's content and / or its style.

Optional Rough Work

Having read Aoife Dooley's article, you have decided to "Sound Off" on some issue about which you have strong views. Write an email to magazine@irishtimes.com expressing your views.

Optional Rough Work

Additional writing space. Label all work clearly with the question number and part.

Additional Writing Space. Label all work clearly with the question number and part.

Additional Writing Space. Label all work clearly with the question number and part.

Acknowledgements

Images
Image on page 59: https://www.flickr.com/photos/jamiefg/8826402736/(21/1/19)
Image on page 62: https://wsimag.com/culture/16119-feminist-poets-think-youre-a-treasure (20/11/18)
Image on page 67: (adapted) https://www.brit.co/infographic-killing-your-creativity-entrepreneur-magazine/ (18/1/19)
Images on page 68: https://www.nobelprize.org; https://pinterest.ie (8/2/19)
Image on page 78: based on image from www.irishtimes.com (18/1/19)
Image on page 80: https://openclipart.org/detail/211209/loud-megaphone-details (8/2/19)

Texts
Durcan, Paul. "Caught Out." Irish writing today, *The Irish Independent*, (2/5/12)
Browning, Robert. *Meeting At Night;* Hughes, Langston. *Harlem;* Coleridge, Samuel. *The Rime of the Ancient Mariner;* Shakespeare, William. *As You Like It;* Pink Floyd. *Granchester Meadows;* The Proclaimers. *I'm Gonna Be.*
Popkin, Gabriel. *New York Times;* https://www.nobelprize.org/prizes/lists/all-nobel-prizes-in-literature
Dooley, Aoife. Sound Off, *The Irish Times*, (11/11/17).

Material may have been adapted, for the purpose of assessment, without the authors' prior consent.

Junior Cycle Final Examination – Higher Level

English

Wednesday 5 June
Morning 9:30 – 11:30

State Examinations Commission

Junior Cycle 2018
Final Examination
English
Higher Level

Wednesday, 6 June – Morning 9:30 to 11:30

180 marks

Examination Number				

Centre Stamp

Cumulative total	
Note: The mark above must equal the mark awarded in the **Total** box.	

For the Examiner only			
Section	Question	Examiner	Adv.
A	1.		
	2.		
	3.		
	4.		
B	5.		
	6.		
	7.		
C	8.		
	9.		
Assessment Task	AT		
Total			

The theme of this examination paper is
Appearance and Reality

Instructions

There are three sections in this examination paper.

Section A	Reading and Writing with Competence	55 marks	4 questions
Section B	Understanding Characters	65 marks	3 questions
Section C	Responding Imaginatively to Texts	60 marks	2 questions

Answer all 9 questions.

The questions do not all carry equal marks. The number of marks for each question is stated at the top of the question.

You should spend about 40 minutes on Section A, 35 minutes on Section B and 40 minutes on Section C.

When answering on studied material, you must use texts in line with what is prescribed for 2018.

Write your answers in the spaces provided in this booklet. You may lose marks if you do not do so. You are not required to use all of the space provided. You should read each question in full before beginning your response.

Extra pages are provided if needed. Label any extra work clearly with the question number and part.

You may only use blue or black pen when writing your answers. Do not use pencil.

Suggested time for Section A: 40 minutes

Read the following text by Tufayel Ahmed from *Newsweek.com* and the accompanying screenshots. Answer the questions that follow.

FACTITIOUS

There is a thin line between *real* news and *fake* news. Even the most vociferous newshound is prone to falling for a deceptive article posted by a friend of a friend that lurks on our Facebook feed. But now you can sharpen your ability to spot fake news and hopefully avoid being duped by fake stories.

Introducing *Factitious*, the web game that tests your knowledge of real and fake news. It's pretty easy for anyone to play. Players have to swipe or click, depending on whether they think the story is true or fake.

Factitious derives its news stories from various sources around the web, some reputable, and some not so reputable. The headlines all sound pretty preposterous— "Hash browns recalled over golf ball bits," reads one—but some are, in fact, true, the hash brown story included.
The online game was created by JoLT, a collaborative at the American University in Washington, D.C., that promotes innovation in journalism through game design.

The concept for *Factitious* comes from Maggie Farley, who worked for 14 years as a journalist at the *Los Angeles Times*. In an interview with *Newsweek,* Farley said she originally devised the game to help middle and high school students discern fake news stories from real news stories.

Farley hopes to rollout the software as a free, open-source learning tool for students and newsrooms. Educators will be able to input their own stories and test their students, which, given the age we're living in, is probably a valuable life skill.

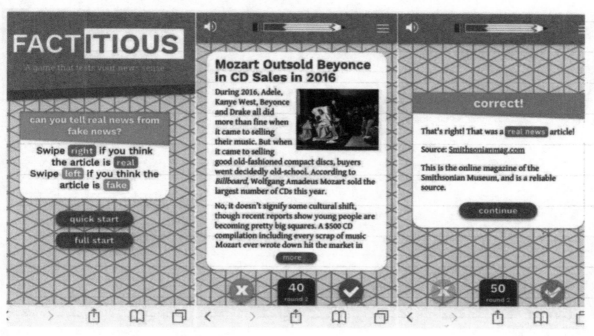

Question 1

Based on your reading of the texts on page three:

- Explain in your own words why the game *Factitious* was developed

- Give reasons why, in your view, the game is or is not useful to young people today.

Optional Rough Work

_____

_____

_____

_____

_____

_____

_____

_____

_____

_____

_____

_____

_____

_____

_____

_____

_____

_____

_____

_____

_____

_____

_____

_____

_____

Question 2   5 marks

The following words, in bold, appear in the passage printed on page three. In the case of each word, indicate what that word means, as it is used in the passage, by placing a tick ✓ in the appropriate box. Tick one box only in each case.

(a)   Duped

        deceived   duplicated   dedicated

        ☐   ☐   ☐

(b)   Reputable

        famous   trustworthy   popular

        ☐   ☐   ☐

(c)   Preposterous

        pompous   sensible   ludicrous

        ☐   ☐   ☐

(d)   Collaborative

  a group working together   something believable   a boring conversation

        ☐   ☐   ☐

(e)   Discern

        reject   talk about   distinguish

        ☐   ☐   ☐

Study the following photograph, taken by Eric Luke and read the accompanying written text by Arminta Wallace, before completing questions three and four.

At first glance... Why did the elephant cross the road?

When I was a kid we used to sing a song which went: "Nellie the elephant packed her trunk and said goodbye to the circus. Off she went with a trumpety-trump: Trump! Trump! Trump!"

In the late 1950s, we did not know much about elephants. We didn't know that they grieve for their dead, or how brutally they are treated by poachers. We didn't know what was coming down the tracks: habitat loss and climate change.

We thought it was fine to have elephants in the circus.

The image above which was originally published on the front page of *The Irish Times* on the last day of 1992, was accompanied by a caption which read:

Trunk and Orderly: Mr Richard Chipperfield exercising the elephants on arrival at the Point Theatre, where the Chipperfield Circus opens on Saturday...

At first glance, it's kind of cute. The young man out for a walk with his pets on a lead. The massive creatures lumbering obediently behind, trunks curled around tails like toddlers holding hands on an outing.

But it's also bleak and sad. Elephants don't belong on tarmac; against the treeless, pitiless background the animals look shabby and ill-groomed.

Between outright and partial bans in the EU, worldwide and closer to home, animal circuses appear to be headed for extinction. It's an emotive subject; if you wish to read something sensible on the matter, try the 'Big Stop' section of the ISPCA's website.

And if you're going to the circus this summer, here's hoping it stars talented human performers, acting as wild as they want to.

Do you think that the writer of this article uses language effectively, to convey her views to the reader? Explain your answer with reference to the article.

```
Optional Rough Work
```

Question 4   **20 Marks**

*It is now against the law for circuses in Ireland to use **wild** animals.*

You are participating in a debate on the motion that: 'The use of **all** animals in circuses should be banned and zoos should be closed down.' You must either agree or disagree with the motion. State and develop any two points you would make to persuade an audience attending the debate that your views are correct.

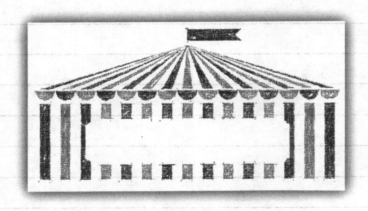

2018

94

Additional Writing Space. Label all work clearly with the question number and part.

Section B   Understanding Characters   65 marks

Suggested time for Section B: 35 minutes

Question 5   **40 marks**

Choose a novel you have studied. To what extent has your understanding of people and human behaviour been shaped by reading this novel? Explain your answer with reference to your chosen text.

Title of novel: _____

Author: _____

Optional Rough Work

_____

_____

_____

_____

_____

_____

_____

_____

_____

_____

_____

Question 6   20 marks

Imagine that one of the following two pictures shows a character from a story that you are writing. In your story, the character is not all that he or she appears to be. Write a descriptive passage that introduces your character to readers. Choose one picture only.

Picture A   **Picture B**

Optional Rough Work

_____

_____

_____

_____

_____

_____

99

_____

_____

_____

_____

_____

_____

_____

_____

_____

_____

_____

_____

_____

_____

_____

Question 7   **5 marks**

In each of the following sentences, one of the homophones used is correct and one is incorrect. In each case circle the **one** homophone that is correct. Homophones are words that sound the same but have different meanings. The first example has been completed for you.

(a) [Two] / too rabbits appeared out of the magician's hat.

(b) The pupils placed there / their coats on hooks and sat down quietly.

(c) I had to alter / altar my costume before the show.

(d) I was not allowed / aloud to swim in the old quarry.

(e) My brother was so proud, he finally passed his test and got his driver's licence / license.

(f) I stood at the end of the pier / peer and watched the sunset.

Additional Writing Space. Label all work clearly with the question number and part.

2018

Section C   Responding Imaginatively to Texts   60 marks

Suggested time for Section C: 40 minutes

Question 8   **45 marks**

(a)   *Conflict is at the centre of all drama.*

From a prescribed Shakespearean play you have studied, select two moments where there is conflict. Discuss how this conflict contributes to making these moments dramatic. Support your response with reference to your chosen moments.   (30)

Title of Shakespearean play: _____

Optional Rough Work

_____

_____

_____

_____

_____

_____

_____

_____

_____

_____

_____

_____

_____

_____

_____

_____

_____

_____

_____

_____

_____

_____

_____

_____

_____

(b)   Choose one of the moments of conflict that you discussed in part **(a)**. In your view, was the conflict that you discussed, resolved satisfactorily in the play? Explain your answer.   (15)

Optional Rough Work

Read the following poem by Edwin Romond and answer the question that follows.

Seeing and Believing

The girls giggled
but the boys laughed right out loud
when Mrs. Stone raged crimson
holding my eighth grade project:
"The Map of New Jersey."
"Get up here, boy!"
and I had no choice
but to walk the gangplank to her desk
where my map choked in her fist.
"What's this jazz? Huh?
The ocean is not green, Bub, it's blue.
Ya' get it? Blue, blue, blue, blue!"
punching my map with each new word into my chest.
My classmates roared a chorus
of "Green ocean! Green ocean!"
their voices rising in waves of laughter
as I carried the wrinkled and ripped map
back to my seat through their sneers.
Soon, all their maps perimetered the room
leaving me adrift in the memory of a Sunday
when, in the October air,
my father and I walked over seashells
and I, only nine,
remarked that the ocean looked green.
My father, peering out from beneath his cap,
said, "Yes, it does" and his fingers swam
through my hair.

Edwin Romond

Question 9   **15 marks**

What aspects of the poem, *Seeing and Believing,* would make it suitable for dramatisation?
Explain your answer with reference to the poem.

Optional Rough Work

Additional Writing Space. Label all work clearly with the question number and part.

Additional Writing Space. Label all work clearly with the question number and part.

2018

Additional Writing Space. Label all work clearly with the question number and part.

Additional Writing Space. Label all work clearly with the question number and part.

2018

Acknowledgements

Images
Images on page 87: http://factitious.augamestudio.com
Image on page 90: Eric Luke, https://www.irishtimes.com
Image on page 92: http://www.ark.ie
Images on page 99: http://www.pinterest.com.au, https://pxhere.com/en/photo/770139
Image on page 106: http://flashlarevista.com/content/boat-on-clear-water.html

Texts
Ahmed, Tufayel. http://www.newsweek.com (4/7/17)
Wallace, Arminta. "At first glance – Why did the elephant cross the road?" *The Irish Times* (22/7/17)
Romond, Edwin. "Seeing and Believing". *Dream Teaching.* Grayson Books, 2005.

Material may have been adapted, for the purpose of assessment, without the authors' prior consent.

Junior Cycle Final Examination – **Higher Level**

English

Wednesday 6 June
Morning 9:30 – 11:30

Coimisiún na Scrúduithe Stáit
State Examinations Commission

Junior Cycle 2017
Final Examination

English

Higher Level

Wednesday, 7 June – Morning 9:30 to 11:30

180 marks

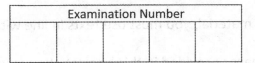

Examination Number

Centre Stamp

Mysteries

Instructions

There are four sections in this examination paper.

Section A	Reading to Analyse and Evaluate	35 marks	2 questions
Section B	Showing Critical Appreciation	45 marks	2 questions
Section C	Appreciating Character, Setting, Story and Action	75 marks	5 questions
Section D	Engaging in the Writing Process	25 marks	1 question

Answer all 10 questions.

The questions do not all carry equal marks. The number of marks for each question is stated at the top of the question.

You should spend about 25 minutes on Section A, 30 minutes on Section B, 45 minutes on Section C and 15 minutes on Section D.

When answering on studied material, you must use texts in line with what is prescribed for 2017.

Write your answers in the spaces provided in this booklet. You may lose marks if you do not do so. You are not required to use all of the space provided.

Extra pages are provided if needed. Label any extra work clearly with the question number and part.

114

Section A	Reading to Analyse and Evaluate	35 marks

The following promotional radio clip is based on the documentary, *Fantastic Beasts and the People who Love Them,* by Shane Dunphy. The full documentary was broadcast as part of the RTÉ Radio, *Documentary on One* series. Read the script and answer the question that follows.

Voice of Continuity Announcer: In tonight's *Documentary on One* series, Shane Dunphy explores the mysterious world of *Cryptozoology* and endeavours to find proof that Ireland's mythical monsters or mystery animals really exist. Here is just a flavour of what you will hear...

Voice of Shane Dunphy: Cryptozoology, for those who don't know, is the study of mystery creatures that may... or may not exist. The evidence about them is either legendary or anecdotal.

Sound Effect: *Haunting screech of an unidentifiable animal.*

Voice of Shane Dunphy: I've been interested in wildlife and nature my whole life. I've swum with seals and dolphins and I've even gone into the mountains to find wild boar.
In 2010 however I met a man called Sean Corcoran, a Waterford-based artist who told me a fantastic story about an encounter he had on Omey Island in Connemara with what was – for want of a better word – a monster.

Voice of Sean Corcoran: ...and there was a bit of an explosion ...and to our absolute shock and horror, a creature of great scale like a giant otter came flying out of the lake turned its head and snarled viciously at us.

Voice of Shane Dunphy: The shove I needed to go in search of Sean's monster came years later and it was my daughter Marnie who gave me that shove...

Voice of Marnie: Why don't you make a documentary where you actually *find* something? I just hate the way there's never any stone-hard evidence …and it's always the same …they are always like…

'What's out there? No one knows!'

Voice of Shane Dunphy: Let's get one thing clear, I'm sceptical. I'd love to believe these things exist but I reckon they are probably misrepresentations and exaggerations in most cases but I wasn't going to let my little girl down. Welcome to the strange world of Irish monster-hunting!

Background Sound Effect: *Calming natural sounds, birdsong, waves crashing.*

Voice of Shane Dunphy: I walk about the lake on Omey. I'm accompanied by birds, meadow pipit and pied wagtail, who follow me as I step from rock to rock. At my back is the constant boom of the sea. It is lonely and it is beautiful but no giant otter puts in an appearance.

Background Sound Effect: *Howling wind.*

The rain comes down over Omey, I run for cover and almost trip over the body of a greater black-backed gull. It had been freshly killed. A fox could not have taken so large and aggressive a bird. The greater black-backed gull can have a wing span of over five feet.

Something much bigger must have taken this bird…

Question 1   15 marks

Based on what you have read in the above script, explain whether you would or you would not like to listen to the entire documentary, *Fantastic Beasts and the People who Love Them*. Refer to aspects of the script to support your response.

Optional Rough Work

Question 2   **20 marks**

Write a critical analysis of the poster below for the film, *Fantastic Beasts & Where To Find Them.*
In it you should consider:
- The visual impact of the poster

and

- Whether or not the poster makes you want to see the film.

2017

| Section B | Showing Critical Appreciation | 45 marks |

Question 3   **40 marks**

(a)   *'The more familiar you become with a poem, the deeper your understanding of that poem becomes.'*

Select a poem you have studied and explain how this statement applies to your understanding of this poem. Use the poem to support your ideas.

Title of poem: _____

Name of poet: _____

(b)   Identify at least two poetic techniques used in your chosen poem and explain how the poet makes effective use of these techniques in this poem. Support your ideas with reference to the poem.

(Rough work and answer space for part **(b)** start on page 12.)

Answer part **(a)**

Optional Rough Work

2017

_____

_____

_____

_____

_____

_____

_____

_____

_____

_____

_____

(Answer for part **(b)** which appears on page 10.)

(Answer for part **(b)** which appears on page 10.)

Optional Rough Work

_____

_____

_____

_____

_____

_____

_____

_____

_____

_____

_____

Question 4   **5 marks**

Indicate whether the use of apostrophes in each of the following sentences is:

Correct   ☑

Or

Incorrect   ☒

   (a)   Paul's collection of poems will be published this summer.   ☐

   (b)   It's difficult for me to understand poems that were written before my time.   ☐

   (c)   The correct use of apostrophe's is a mystery to me.   ☐

   (d)   The sun was magnificent, it's rays were sparkling on the waves.   ☐

   (e)   Five students' poems will be printed in the next newsletter.   ☐

Additional Writing Space. Label all work clearly with the question number and part.

Section C   Appreciating Character, Setting, Story and Action   75 marks

Read the text printed below and the extract from Shakespeare's play, *The Tempest*. Answer the questions which follow

> ### The Background
>
> **Prospero**, Duke of Milan, was expelled from his Dukedom by his brother **Antonio**. He finds refuge on an island. Prospero has magical powers that allow him to control spirits, humans and the elements. An opportunity presents itself for Prospero to get revenge, when Antonio arrives on the same island. Antonio is in the company of Alonso, the King of Naples.
>
> The characters:
> - **Alonso,** King of Naples
> - **Ferdinand**, King Alonso's son
> - **Sebastian,** King Alonso's brother
> - **Antonio,** Prospero's scheming brother
> - **Gonzalo**, an honest old courtier
> - **Prospero,** former Duke of Milan (a magician).

> As the extract opens, Alonso and his companions are searching the island for Ferdinand, who is missing. Antonio and Sebastian are plotting to kill Alonso.
>
> Prospero controls events from above. The audience can see Prospero but the other characters on stage cannot see him.
>
> Magically, Prospero makes a procession of spirits appear. They bring a banquet of food. Dancing around a table, they invite the weary travellers to eat. Just as the travellers attempt to taste the food, Prospero makes the banquet disappear.

Enter *Alonso, Sebastian, Antonio, Gonzalo, and others.*

Gonzalo.   I can go no further, sir;
    My old bones ache; here's a maze trod indeed
    Through meandering paths! By your patience,
    I needs must rest me.

Alonso.   Old lord, I cannot blame thee,
    Who am myself seized with weariness,
    Sit down and rest.
    Even here I will put off my hope, and keep it
    No longer: Ferdinand is dead
    Whom thus we stray to find, and nature mocks   10
    Our frustrated search on this island. Well, let him go.

Antonio.   *[To Sebastian]* I am right glad that he's so out of hope.
    Do not, for one repulse, forgo the purpose
    That you resolved to effect.*   * to kill Alonso

Sebastian.   *[To Antonio]* The next advantage we will take thoroughly.

Antonio.   *[To Sebastian]* Let it be to-night
    For, now they are oppressed with travel, they
    Will not, nor cannot, use such vigilance
    As when they are fresh.

Sebastian.   *[To Antonio]* I say to-night: no more.   20

    Solemn and strange music; enter Prospero above, invisible to the other
    characters. Enter several strange Spirits, bringing in a banquet; they dance about it
    with gentle actions of salutation, inviting Alonso, etc., to eat.

Alonso.   What harmony is this? My good friends, hark!

Gonzalo.   Marvellous sweet music!

Alonso.   Give us kind keepers, heavens! What were these?

Gonzalo.   If in Naples
    I should report this now, would they believe me?
    Who, though they are of monstrous shape, yet
    Their manners are more gentle-kind, you shall find,
    Than many of our human generation.

    The strange Spirits depart.

Prospero.   *[Aside]* Honest lord,
    Thou hast said well; for some of you there present   30
    Are worse than devils.

Alonso.	I cannot too much muse
	Such shapes, such gesture, and such sound, expressing
	(Although they want the use of tongue) a kind
	Of excellent dumb discourse.
Prospero.	*[Aside]* Keep your praise till the end.
Antonio.	They vanish'd strangely.
Sebastian.	No matter, since
	They have left the banquet behind; for we have stomachs -
	Will't please you taste of what is here? 40

Alonso.	Not I.
Gonzalo.	Faith sir, you need not fear. When we were boys,
	Who would believe that there were such creatures,
	Dew-lapp'd like bulls, whose throats had hanging at 'em
	Wallets of flesh? Yet now we find
	Explorers bring us proof of.
Alonso.	I will stand to, and feed.

Thunder and lightning. As if by magic, the banquet vanishes.

Question 5   **10 marks**

In the case of each of the following, write the letter corresponding to the correct answer in the appropriate box.

(a) Which word best describes Alonso's mood at the start of the extract?
(Lines 5-11)

   A. Relieved

   B. Aggressive

   C. Disconsolate

(b) Based on what you have read in the text and the extract above, which of the following characters are both villains?

   A. Alonso and Gonzalo

   B. Gonzalo and Antonio

   C. Antonio and Sebastian

(c) Which one of the following is the best explanation of the lines,

> *... they are oppressed with travel, they*
> *Will not, nor cannot, use such vigilance*
> *As when they are fresh.* (Lines 17-19)?

A. They are anxious to continue their journey.

B. They are so tired that they can be easily caught off-guard.

C. With the Spirits' help they are now prepared for anything.

(d) Which one of the following is the best explanation of the lines,

> *I cannot too much muse*
> *Such shapes, such gesture, and such sound, expressing*
> *(Although they want the use of tongue) a kind*
> *Of excellent dumb discourse.* (Lines 32-35)?

A. It's remarkable how these forms can say so much without the use of speech.

B. I don't want to think about what I have just seen.

C. I do not understand what these creatures mean at all.

(e) *Asides* are used by Prospero in this extract. What is an aside?

A. A position for an actor on the extreme left or right of the stage.

B. Thoughts spoken out loud, largely for the benefit of the audience.

C. A group of characters who comment on the action in a drama.

Question 6 **20 marks**

The magical world depicted in *The Tempest,* creates opportunities for a director to stage the play in an imaginative way.

Based on your reading of the above extract from *The Tempest* (Pages 17-18), explain **two** things a director could do to stage this extract from the play in an imaginative way.

Optional Rough Work

_____

_____

_____

_____

_____

_____

_____

_____

_____

_____

_____

_____

Question 8   20 marks

Choose one of the qualities identified in your list above. Explain how at least two key moments
in the play highlight this quality in your chosen character. Use your knowledge of the play to
justify your viewpoints.

Question 7   **5 marks**

Select one character from a Shakespearean play you have studied and list five adjectives that
identify this character's essential qualities.

Title of play: _____

Name of character: _____

List of Adjectives
(a)_____
(b)_____
(c)_____
(d)_____
(e)_____

Question 8

Choose **one** of the qualities identified in your list above. Explain how at least two key moments from the play highlight this quality in your chosen character. Use your knowledge of the play to justify your viewpoints.

Optional Rough Work

_____

_____

_____

_____

_____

_____

_____

_____

_____

_____

_____

A film version is being made of the Shakespearean play you have studied. What would you include on a poster advertising the film, to represent what you think is important in the play and to create a sense of anticipation for its opening release? Explain your answer with reference to the play.

Optional Rough Work

A film version is being made of the Shakespearean play you have studied. What would you include on a poster advertising the film, to represent what you think is important in the play and to create a sense of anticipation for its upcoming release? Explain your decisions with reference to the play.

Optional Rough Work

2017

Additional Writing Space. Label all work clearly with the question number and part.

Question 10   **25 marks**

Study the Word Cloud printed below. Complete the task that follows.

Why can't you be like...?

Wet towel pile on bathroom floor Up all night, in bed all day

"There's never anything to eat in this house" **Storming out of the room**

You're a complete Mystery to me

You're not going out wearing that **YOU JUST** MMS (Major Mood Swing) **DON'T GET IT**

"Everyone else is going …"

Cheeky **Yeah Right** "You just don't understand me"

How could you? Totally empty fridge – again Door Slam

Your room is a pig sty! "Whatever" **SO embarrassing!**

Grunt Mouldy plates and mugs in bedroom

Facebook activity at 3 am

Texting at the table Barefaced lie **Eye Roll** Used up all the hot water

Shoes EVERYWHERE "I hate you"

Compulsive selfie taking Treat this place like a hotel

Every single light in the house switched on and left on

Totally silent car journey involving headphone use

Overflowing laundry basket

2017

Using one or more of the words or phrases from the Word Cloud above, write the dialogue for a scene in a TV drama where an adult confronts a teenager **or** a teenager confronts an adult. Your dialogue may be serious or humorous or both. You may refer to location, the use of special effects and make suggestions for movement in your script. Indicate each speaker on the left-hand side of the page.

Optional Rough Work

Question number	Write the question numbers in the left-hand margin

Question number	Write the question numbers in the left-hand margin

Acknowledgements

Images

Images on page 115: privateislandparty.com (10/1/17); pinterest.com (9/3/17)
Image on page 118: warnerbros.com
Image on page 128: music.usc.edu (26/1/17)
Image on page 133: biography.com (30/1/17)
Image on page 139: State Examinations Commission

Texts
Shane Dunphy, *Fantastic Beasts and the People who Love Them.* Transcript from RTÉ, *Documentary on One*
William Shakespeare, *The Tempest* (Arden)

Material may have been adapted, for the purpose of assessment, without the authors' prior consent.

Junior Cycle 2017
Final Examination

English
Higher Level

Wednesday 7 June
Morning 9:30 to 11:30

Edco has reprinted the edited transcript in Section A by kind permission of: *'Documentary On One, RTÉ Radio 1 Fantastic Beasts and the People who Love Them'* http://www.rte.ie/radio1/doconone/education/

Coimisiún na Scrúduithe Stáit
State Examinations Commission

Junior Cycle 20XX
Final Examination Sample 2

English

Higher Level

Day Date June – Morning 9:30 to 11:30

180 marks

Examination number

Centre Stamp

SEC SAMPLE 2

The theme of this examination paper is
Making Connections

Instructions

There are **two** sections in this examination paper.

Section A   Reading Texts to Understand – Shakespearean Drama   80 marks   5 questions
Section B   Responding to Texts – Appreciation of Language   100 marks   6 questions

Answer all eleven questions.

The questions do not all carry equal marks. The number of marks for each question is stated at the top of the question.
You should spend about fifty-five minutes on Section A and about fifty-five minutes on Section B.
When answering on studied material, you must use texts prescribed for examination in 201X.

Write your answers in the spaces provided in this booklet. You may lose marks if you do not do so. Space is provided for extra work. Label any extra work clearly with the question number and part.

Section A   Reading Texts to Understand – Shakespearean Drama

The soliloquy printed on page 36 of this booklet is taken from the comedy *Twelfth Night*, by William Shakespeare. Read the background and the soliloquy and answer the questions.

Background to the extract:

Twelfth Night is a comedy based around disguise, confused identity and a complicated love triangle. **Viola**, shipwrecked on the Isle of Illyria disguises herself as a boy called **Cesario**. **Orsino**, the Duke of Illyria employs Cesario to try to help him to woo a wealthy countess named **Olivia** who has vowed not to fall in love with anyone for seven years. When Cesario is sent with a message from Orsino to Olivia, things get complicated.

- Orsino is in love with the Countess Olivia, who has rejected his approaches.
- Cesario (Viola) is sent by Orsino to woo Olivia on his behalf.
- Olivia rejects Orsino's suit but falls in love with Cesario not realising that "he" is really a woman (Viola).
- Viola is secretly in love with her new employer Orsino.

Question 1   5 marks

Match the character to the description.

Characters

A.   Viola

B.   Olivia

C.   Orsino

D.   Cesario

E.   Cesario / Viola

Description	Character
The Duke of Illyria who is in love with a countess	
A boy who is really a woman in disguise	
A woman who pretends to be a man and who is secretly in love with her employer	
The same person	
A countess who falls in love with the Duke's messenger	

Extract (soliloquy)

Just before the soliloquy, Cesario (Viola) leaves Olivia's house. She is followed by Olivia's servant who delivers a ring to her on her mistress's behalf. The servant rudely throws the ring on the ground and departs.

Some of the words in the extract are explained in footnotes below.

Viola, alone on the stage, addresses the audience as she works through her confusion.

... Picking up the ring
I left no ring with her: what means this lady?
Fortune forbid my outside have not charm'd her!
She made good view of me; indeed, so much,
That sure methought her eyes hath lost her tongue[1],
For she did speak in starts distractedly.
She loves me, sure; the cunning of her passion
Invites me in this churlish messenger[2].
None of my lord's ring! Why, he sent her none.
I am the man: if it be so, as 'tis,
Poor lady, she were better love a dream.   10
Disguise, I see thou art a wickedness,
Wherein the pregnant enemy[3] does much,
How easy is it for the proper-false
In women's waxen hearts to set their forms!
Alas, our weakness is the cause, not we!
For such as we are made of, such we be.
How will this fadge[4]? My master loves her dearly:
And I, poor monster, fond as much on him:
And she, mistaken, seems to dote on me.
What will become of this? As I am man,   20
My state is desperate for my master's love[5]
As I am woman – now alas the day!
What thriftless sighs shall poor Olivia breathe!
O time! Thou must untangle this, not I;
It is too hard a knot for me to untie!

Exit

---

[1] Looked so closely, she was speechless
[2] Rude servant
[3] Clever enemy
[4] Turn out
[5] Disguised as a man I have no hope of winning my master's love

Question 2

In each case, write the letter corresponding to the correct answer in the box.

(a) Why does Olivia send her servant after Viola/Cesario with the ring?

    A. She does not wish to accept any gifts from Orsino.

    B. She genuinely believes Cesario gave it to her during "his" visit to her house and wants to return it.

    C. She has fallen in love with Cesario and is trying to woo 'him'.

(b) Which of the following is the best re-wording of the lines,
How easy is it for the proper-false
In women's waxen hearts to set their forms. (lines 13-14)?

    A. Men who are false are rejected by clever women.

    B. Women are deceivers and have hard hearts.

    C. Women are impressionable so it is easy for someone who is deceitful and good-looking to manipulate them.

(c) Which of these ideas does the metaphor in the final line support?

    A. It is a straightforward situation and Viola will deal with it herself.

    B. Viola is unable to solve the problem herself.

    C. Viola will turn to Olivia to solve the problem.

(d) What form is the soliloquy written in?

    A. Blank verse

    B. Rhyming couplets

    C. Prose

(e) When Viola says that Olivia will be breathing 'thriftless sighs', what does she mean?

    A. Olivia's sorrow will prove to be costly.

    B. Olivia's sighs are pointless.

    C. Olivia's sighs are laughable.

Question 3   10 marks

You are performing the soliloquy printed on page 36 in your classroom and decide to project one of the following images on to a wall, as background to your performance.

Image A

Image B

Image C

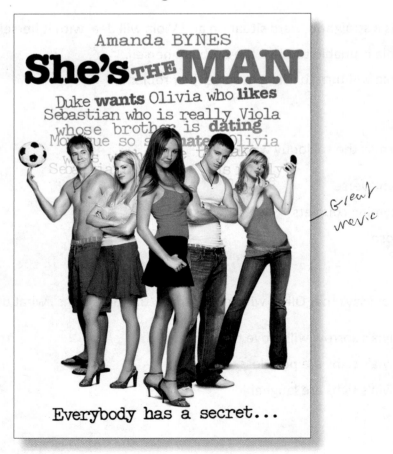

— Great movie

(a) Which of the three images would you use?

(b) What impact do you think this image would have on the way an audience might respond to a performance of the soliloquy?

Optional Rough Work

Question 4

Explain **two** things that you would do in your performance of the soliloquy, in order to make the experience engaging for an audience.

You may refer to both the soliloquy and your chosen image in your response.

Optional Rough Work

Question 5   **40 marks**

Making Connections – Soliloquy or Monologue in a Play I have Studied

Choose a Shakespearean play you have studied where a character delivers a soliloquy or monologue.

(a)   Title of play: _____

Name of character that delivers the soliloquy or monologue: _____

Optional Rough Work

(b)   Describe the situation that occurred, prior to the soliloquy or monologue, which gave rise to the character's thoughts.

_____

_____

_____

_____

_____

_____

_____

_____

_____

_____

_____

_____

(c) Give an account of the thoughts revealed to the audience by this character in the soliloquy or monologue.

_____

_____

_____

_____

_____

_____

_____

_____

_____

_____

_____

_____

_____

_____

_____

_____

_____

_____

_____

(d) Write a letter to the character who delivers the soliloquy or monologue in which you explain how the speech influenced your thoughts and feelings towards that character.

You may refer to other parts of the play.

_____

_____

_____

_____

_____

_____

_____

_____

_____

_____

_____

_____

_____

_____

_____

_____

_____

_____

_____

_____

_____

_____

_____

Additional Writing Space. Label all work clearly with the question number and part

Section B	Responding to Texts – Appreciation of Language.
	Beginnings and Endings in Fiction

The beginnings of three novels are presented below.

The endings of the same three novels, plus one additional ending, are on the next page.
The endings are not necessarily in the same order as the beginnings.

Read all of the beginnings and endings and then answer the questions that follow.

Beginnings

Beginning A

Some people used to believe that there was an elephant graveyard – a place that sick and old
elephants would travel to die. They'd slip away from their herds and would lumber across the
dusty landscape, like the titans we read about in seventh grade in Greek Mythology. Legend said
the spot was in Saudi Arabia; that it was the source of a supernatural force; that it contained a
book of spells to bring about world peace. Explorers who went in search of the graveyard would
follow dying elephants for weeks, only to realise they'd been led in circles. Some of these voyagers
disappeared completely. Some could not remember what they had seen, and not a single explorer
who claimed to have found the graveyard could ever locate it again.
Here's why: the elephant graveyard is a myth.

Beginning B

He was an old man who fished alone in a skiff in the Gulf Stream and he had gone eighty-four
days now without taking a fish. In the first forty days a boy had been with him. But after forty days
without a fish the boy's parents had told him that the old man was now definitely and finally salao,
which is the worst form of unlucky, and the boy had gone at their orders in another boat which
caught three good fish the first week. It made the boy sad to see the old man come in each day
with the skiff empty and he always went down to help him carry either the coiled lines or the gaff
and harpoon and the sail that was furled around the mast. The sail was patched with flour sacks
and, furled, it looked like the flag of permanent defeat.

Beginning C

MAE MOBLEY was born on a early Sunday morning in August 1960. A church baby we like to call
it. Taking care a white babies, that's what I do, along with all the cooking and the cleaning. I done
raised seventeen kids in my lifetime. I know how to get them babies to sleep, stop crying, and go in
the toilet bowl before they mamas even get out abed in the morning.

Endings

Ending 1

That afternoon there was a party of tourists at the terrace and looking down in the water among the empty beer cans and dead barracudas a woman saw a great long white spine with a huge tail at the end that lifted and swung with the tide while the east wind blew a heavy steady sea outside the entrance to the harbour.

'What's that?' she asked a waiter and pointed to the long back bone of the great fish.

'Tiburon,' the waiter said, 'Shark.' He was meaning to explain what had happened.

'I didn't know sharks had such handsome beautifully formed tails.'

Up the road, in his shack, the old man was sleeping again. He was still sleeping on his face and the boy was sitting by him watching him. The old man was dreaming about the lions.

Ending 2

The sun is bright but my eyes is wide open. I stand at the bus stop like I been doing for forty-odd years. In thirty minutes, my whole life's done. Maybe I ought to keep writing, not just for the paper, but something else, about all the people I know and the things I seen and done. Maybe I ain't too old to start over, I think and I laugh and I cry at the same time at this. Cause just last night I thought I was finished with everything new.

Ending 3

When Lawrence Anthony died, the two herds travelled through the Zululand bush for more than half a day and stood outside the wall that bordered his property. They had not been near the house in over a year. The elephants stayed for two days, silent, bearing witness.

No one can explain how the elephants knew that Anthony had died.

I know the answer.

If you think about someone you've loved and lost, you are already with them. The rest is just details.

Ending 4

Then he was gone, walking slowly round the shore in the half-light. The Ruttledges did not speak as they climbed the hill.

'What are you going to do?' Kate asked as they passed beneath the alder tree.

'I'm not sure.' he said. 'We can talk it through. We don't have to decide on anything till morning.'

At the porch, before entering the house, they both turned to look back across the lake, even though they knew that both Jamesie and Mary had long since disappeared from the sky.

Question 6   **6 marks**

For each of the three beginnings, select which of the endings (1, 2, 3, or 4) you think is the correct one.

Beginning	Ending
A	
B	
C	

Question 7   **16 marks**

In the case of beginning **B** and beginning **C**, justify your selection, based on both the **content** and **style** of each extract.

Optional Rough Work

Beginning **B** – justification of chosen ending:

_____

_____

_____

_____

_____

_____

_____

_____

_____
_____
_____
_____
_____
_____
_____

_____
_____
_____
_____

Beginning C – justification of chosen ending: _____
_____
_____
_____
_____
_____
_____
_____
_____
_____
_____
_____
_____

Question 8   **10 marks**

The following words appear in the passages printed on pages 45 and 46: *Lumber, Furled, Witness, Legend, Terrace.* Write a definition of each word **as it is used in its passage.**

Lumber *[beginning **A**, second line]*: _____

_____

_____

Furled *[beginning **B**, last line]*: _____

_____

_____

Witness *[ending **3**, third line]*: _____

_____

_____

Legend *[beginning **A**, third line]*: _____

_____

_____

Terrace *[ending **1**, first line]*: _____

_____

_____

Question 9   **18 marks**

(a)   List any three characteristics that you believe are important for a good opening to a novel.

1. _____

_____

2. _____

_____

3. _____

_____

(b) List any three characteristics that you believe are important for a good ending to a novel.

1. _____

_____

_____

2. _____

_____

_____

3. _____

_____

_____

Question 10   **40 marks**

Using the criteria that you suggested in **(a)** and **(b)** above, write an assessment of the opening and closing sections of any novel you studied as part of your coursework.

Title of text: _____

Author: _____

```
                          Optional Rough Work




```

Assessment of opening:

Assessment of ending:

Question 11   10 marks

Using the image below as a prompt, write an **opening** paragraph for a story. Suggest a title for your story.

Optional Rough Work

Story title:

_____

_____

_____

Opening paragraph:

Additional Writing Space. Label all work clearly with the question number and part.

Additional Writing Space. Label all work clearly with the question number and part.

Additional Writing Space. Label all work clearly with the question number and part.

SEC SAMPLE 2

Additional Writing Space. Label all work clearly with the question number and part.

Additional Writing Space. Label all work clearly with the question number and part.

Acknowledgments

Images

Image on page 147: myblog-inplainenglish.blogspot.com
Images on page 148: masktheatre.co.uk; 116ameyer.wordpress.com
Images on page 150: waukeshasivictheatre.org; marsroses.com; elizabethfais.com
Image on page 157: sa.uca.org.au
Image on page 165: gettyimages.lu

Texts

Shakespeare, William. *Twelfth Night*, Ed Keir Elam, London: Methuen, 2008.
Stockett, Kathyrn. *The Help*, New York: Penguin, 2009.
Hemingway, Ernest. *The Old Man and the Sea*, New York: Charles Scribner's, 1952.
Picoult, Jodi. *Leaving Time*, New York: Ballantine Books, 2014.
Mc Gahern, John. *That They May Face the Rising Sun*. Dublin: Faber and Faber, 2001.

Texts may have been adapted, for the purpose of assessment, without the authors' prior consent.

Junior Cycle 20XX
Final Examination Sample 2

English
Higher Level

Edco has reprinted extracts in Section B by kind permission:
From *'The Old Man and the Sea'* by Ernest Hemingway. Published by Jonathan Cape. Reprinted by permission of the Random House Group Ltd.
From *'The Help'* by Kathryn Stockett, © 2009 by Kathryn Stockett. Used by permission of GP Putnam's Sons, an imprint of Penguin Publishing Group, a division of Penguin Random House LLC.
From *Leaving Time* by Jodi Picoult. By kind permission of Jodi Picoult.
'That They May Face the Rising Sun' by John McGahern © Faber and Faber.

Wednesday X June
Morning 9:30 to 11:30

Coimisiún na Scrúduithe Stáit
State Examinations Commission

Junior Cycle 20XX
Final Examination Sample 3

English

Higher Level

Day Date June – Morning 9:30 to 11:30

180 marks

Examination number

Centre Stamp

SEC SAMPLE 3

The theme of this examination paper is
A Sense of Place

Instructions

There are **four** sections in this examination paper.

Section A	Appreciating Audience and Register	30 marks	2 questions
Section B	Responding to Studied Texts	50 marks	2 questions
Section C	Reading Comprehension Strategies	20 marks	3 questions
Section D	Appreciating Language	80 marks	5 questions

Answer all twelve questions.

The questions do not all carry equal marks. The number of marks for each question is stated at the top of the question.

You should spend about twenty-five minutes on Sections A and B, fifteen minutes on Section C and forty-five minutes on Section D.

When answering on studied material, you must use texts prescribed for examination in 201X.

Write your answers in the spaces provided in this booklet. You may lose marks if you do not do so. Space is provided for extra work. Label any extra work clearly with the question number and part

Section A Appreciating Audience and Register – Faraway Places

Read the following passage. It is taken from a talk given by NASA astronaut, Commander Chris Hadfield. Complete the task that follows. The passage is written to reflect the way in which the talk was delivered to a live audience.

SEC SAMPLE 3

Question 1   **20 marks**

In your view, what elements of the above talk would have made it engaging for the audience listening? Explain your answer by referring to both the style and the content of the talk.

Optional Rough Work

Question 2   **10 marks**

The pictures below show the settings for three different stories. Choose **one** of the pictures and
write a descriptive paragraph in which you create a picture of the place and give the reader a sense
of the mood or atmosphere in that place.

(a) Exploring Mars

(b) Undiscovered

(c) Boundaries

I choose to set my story in the place shown in the picture labelled: _____

Descriptive Paragraph:

```
                        Optional Rough Work




```

_____

_____

_____

_____

_____

_____

_____

_____

_____

_____

_____

_____

_____

_____

_____

_____

_____

Additional Writing Space. Label all work clearly with the question number and part.

In the boxes provided below give the titles and authors of two of the novels you have studied on your course. Marks are awarded for giving full titles and names with correct spelling.

First Novel	Second Novel
Title:	Title:
Author:	Author:

Question 3   **25 marks**

Compare the settings of your two chosen novels using the three following headings to guide your response: Physical Location; Mood or Atmosphere; Social Values.

Optional Rough Work

SEC SAMPLE 3

Choose one important character from each of the two novels you have selected above.

Name of character from first novel:	Name of character from second novel:

Question 4 25 marks

Which one of your chosen characters was more influenced by the world that he or she lived in? Explain your answer giving examples. Refer to both of your chosen characters in your answer.

Optional Rough Work

Additional Writing Space. Label all work clearly with the question number and part.

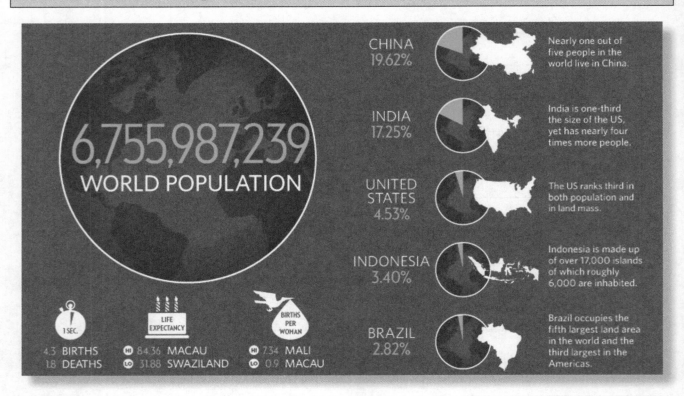

Question 5   **5 marks**

Study the above info-graphic on world population carefully then complete the following sentences using only the information provided.

(a)   The country with the greatest number of people living in it is: _____

(b)   The birth rate per woman in the Republic of Ireland is 2.01. A country on the info-graphic with a birth rate more than three times the rate in the Republic of Ireland is:

_____

(c)   A country referred to in the info-graphic, with a low average life expectancy is:

_____

(d)   The info-graphic suggests that overall the population of the world is decreasing. Write either T for true or F for false in the box provided

(e)   India is more densely populated than the United States. Write either T for true or F for false in the box provided.

Study the screen-shot from a White House blog below and answer the following questions.

BRIEFING ROOM   ISSUES   THE ADMINISTRATION   PARTICIPATE   1600 PENN

HOME · BLOG

Bringing Our Immigration System into the Digital Age

JULY 15, 2015 AT 3:00 PM ET BY CECILIA MUÑOZ, MIKEY DICKERSON

Summary: Federal agencies are undertaking new actions to improve the visa experience for families, workers, employers, and people in need of humanitarian relief.

In November, President Obama announced a series of Executive Actions to fix the broken immigration system. As a part of these efforts, he charged the key federal agencies responsible for administering our legal immigration system to explore ways to modernize and streamline the system. The goal was to develop recommendations to bring the system into the 21st century to grow our economy, help businesses and workers, and protect families.

Today, we are taking the next step in this effort, releasing a report on *Modernizing and Streamlining Our Legal Immigration System for the 21st Century*. This report includes a wide range of new actions that federal agencies will undertake to improve the visa experience for families, workers, employers, and people in need of humanitarian relief.

Question 6   5 marks

(a)   Identify two digital elements used in the above blog.

Digital Element 1	Digital Element 2

(b)   How can the use of digital elements, like the ones you have identified above, lead to more effective communication of information? You may refer to the above blog and / or other sources in your answer.

_____

_____

_____

_____

_____

_____

_____

_____

Question 7   **10 marks**

The Department of Foreign Affairs is holding a competition inviting secondary school students to devise **two** guidelines that will help newly-arrived immigrants to adjust to living in Ireland.

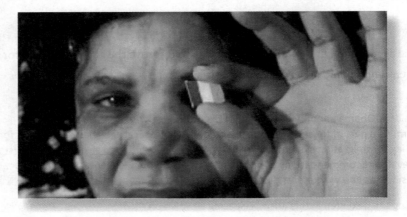

It is intended that the guidelines will be printed on government publications like information leaflets and posters.

In the space provided below, clearly state each guideline, suggest an image that would be appropriate to accompany each guideline and give a reason for both your choice of guideline and its accompanying image.

Guideline (a): _____

_____

Image: _____

_____

Reason: _____

_____

_____

_____

_____

_____

_____

Guideline (b): _____

_____

Image: _____

_____

Reason: _____

_____

_____

_____

_____

_____

_____

Additional Writing Space. Label all work clearly with the question number and part.

_____

_____

_____

_____

_____

_____

_____

_____

_____

_____

_____

_____

_____

_____

_____

Section D   Appreciating Language – Poetry – Inspired by Place

Read the following poem by Seamus Heaney and
answer the questions that follow:

Lovers on Aran

The timeless waves, bright, sifting, broken glass,
Came dazzling around, into the rocks,
Came glinting, sifting from the Americas

To possess Aran.
Or did Aran rush
to throw wide arms of rock around a tide
That yielded with an ebb, with a soft crash?

Did sea define the land or land the sea?
Each drew new meaning from the waves' collision.

Sea broke on land to full identity.

Question 8   20 marks

Identify a line or phrase in the poem where the poet uses each of the following poetic techniques
and explain why you think the poet uses the technique:

Contrast: _____

_____

_____

_____

_____

Personification: _____

_____

_____

SEC SAMPLE 3

Tone: _____

_____

_____

_____

_____

Assonance: _____

_____

_____

_____

Enjambment: _____

_____

_____

_____

Question 9   10 marks

What do you think is the message in this poem? Explain your answer.

_____

_____

_____

_____

_____

_____

_____

_____

_____

Question 10　　　　　　　　　　　　　　　　　　　　　　　**10 marks**

Evaluate how one of the poetic techniques named in Question 8 of this section, helps to convey the message you have identified in the poem.

Optional Rough Work

_____

_____

_____

_____

_____

_____

_____

_____

_____

_____

_____

_____

_____

_____

Question 11　　　　　　　　　　　　　　　　　　　　　　　**30 marks**

Choose any two poems you have studied that you feel give you a strong sense of the places they are set in.

Give the poets' names and the titles of their poems.
Marks are awarded for giving full titles and names with correct spelling.

Title Poem 1:	Title poem 2:
Poet's name:	Poet's name:

In your view, which one of the poets was more successful in conveying a sense of place in his / her poem? Support your analysis with detailed reference to both of your nominated poems.

Question 12   **10 marks**

(a)   Imagine you are writing a poem. Outline the message you would like to convey in your poem.
      The poem could be about something personal, social, universal or a combination of all three.

_____

_____

_____

_____

_____

_____

_____

_____

_____

_____

(b)   Suggest an image you would use in your poem as outlined above and explain why you feel
      that it would be an appropriate image to use.

_____

_____

_____

_____

_____

_____

_____

_____

_____

_____

_____

_____

Additional Writing Space. Label all work clearly with the question number and part.

Additional Writing Space. Label all work clearly with the question number and part.

Additional Writing Space. Label all work clearly with the question number and part.

Acknowledgments

Images

Image on page 175: shutterstock.com
Images on page 178: uk2.net; iwallhd.com; geographyfieldwork.com
Image on page 186: e-whiz.com
Image on page 187: whitehouse.gov/blog
Image on page 188: irishtimes.ie
Images on page 191: thejournal.ie; galway.net; aranislands.ie

Texts

THeaney, Seamus. "Lovers on Aran", Death of a Naturalist, London: Faber and Faber, 1966.
Hadfield, Chris. *Ted Talks*. <http://ted.com/talks/Chris_Hadfield (Accessed 15 September 2015)

Texts may have been adapted, for the purpose of assessment, without the authors' prior consent.

Junior Cycle 20XX
Final Examination Sample 3

English
Higher Level

Wednesday X June
Morning 9:30 to 11:30

Junior Cycle 20XX
Final Examination Sample A

English

Higher Level

Day Date June – Morning 9:30 to 11:30

180 marks

Examination number

The theme of this examination paper is
Reading and Writing

Instructions

There are **four** sections in this examination paper.

Section A	Showing Critical Appreciation	50 marks	4 questions
Section B	Reading and Responding to Texts	50 marks	3 questions
Section C	Appreciating Poetry	40 marks	1 question
Section D	Creating Stories	40 marks	2 questions

Answer all 10 questions.

The questions do not all carry equal marks. The number of marks for each question is stated at the top of the question.

You should spend about 35 minutes on Section A
You should spend about 40 minutes on Section B
You should spend about 20 minutes on Section C
You should spend about 20 minutes on Section D

When answering on studied material, you must use texts prescribed for examination in 20XX.

Write your answers in the spaces provided in this booklet. You may lose marks if you do not do so. Space is provided for extra work. Label any extra work clearly with the question number and part.

You may only use blue or black pen when writing your answers. Do not use pencil.

The examination booklet will be scanned and your work will be presented to an examiner on screen. Anything that you write outside of the answer areas may not be seen by the examiner.

Suggested time for Section A: 35 minutes

Read the poem by Julia Donaldson and answer the questions which follow.

I Opened a Book

I opened a book and in I strode.
Now nobody can find me.
I've left my chair, my house, my road,
My town and my world behind me.

I'm wearing the cloak, I've slipped on the ring,
I've swallowed the magic potion.
I've fought with a dragon, dined with a king
And dived in a bottomless ocean.

I opened a book and made some friends.
I shared their tears and laughter
And followed their road with its bumps and bends
To the happily ever after.

I finished my book and out I came.
The cloak can no longer hide me.
My chair and my house are just the same,
But I have a book inside me.

Question 1   **(10 marks)**

Optional Rough Work

What do you think the poet means when she says, "I opened a book and in I strode"?

_____

_____

_____

_____

_____

_____

Question 2   **(15 marks)**

Identify **two** features of the writing that you think enrich the language of the poem. Explain your choices.

Optional Rough Work

Question 3 (5 marks)

Choose from the list of literary terms in **bold** below to complete the table by matching the term to the **most appropriate** lines of poetry. The first example is completed for you. (Use each term only once.)

Metaphor   Alliteration   Rhyme   Simile   Rhetorical Question   Enjambment

I opened a book and in I strode	Metaphor
At his still firm shoulder, I rest for a while in the shade, not looking down	
And followed their road with its bumps and bends	
the hair flapping behind you like a handkerchief waving goodbye.	
Is your life more real because you dig and sow?	
And charging along like troops in a battle, All through the meadows the horses and cattle:	

Question 4 (20 marks)

Read parts **(a)** and **(b)** carefully before writing your answers in the appropriate spaces below.

(a) *Some films make you feel that you have shared in the life of the central character.*

Select a film you have studied and explain why you felt you shared in the life of the central character. Refer to the film to support your answer.

(b) Do you think the film explored themes that were relevant to viewers of your age? Explain your answer, supporting your response with reference to the film.

Title of film: _____

Name of director: _____

```
Optional Rough Work




```

Answer space for part (a)

_____

_____

_____

_____

_____

_____

_____

_____

_____

_____

_____

_____

_____

Optional Rough Work

Answer space for part (b)

_____

_____

_____

_____

_____

_____

_____

_____

_____

_____

_____

_____

_____

_____

_____

_____

_____

_____

_____

_____

_____

Suggested Time for Section B: 40 minutes

Read the following text and answer question 5. The passage is taken from a talk given by children's author Neil Gaiman. The theme of the talk is the importance of reading.

We have an obligation to read aloud to our children. To read them things they enjoy. To read to them stories we are already tired of. To do the voices, to make it interesting, and not to stop reading to them just because they learn to read to themselves. Use reading-aloud time as bonding time, as time when no phones are being checked, when the distractions of the world are put aside.

We have an obligation to use the language. To push ourselves: to find out what words mean and how to deploy them, to communicate clearly, to say what we mean. We must not attempt to freeze language, or to pretend it is a dead thing that must be revered, but we should use it as a living thing, that flows, that borrows words, that allows meanings and pronunciations to change with time.

We writers – and especially writers for children, but all writers – have an obligation to our readers: it's the obligation to write true things, especially important when we are creating tales of people who do not exist in places that never were – to understand that truth is not in what happens but what it tells us about who we are. Fiction is the lie that tells the truth, after all. We have an obligation not to bore our readers, but to make them need to turn the pages. One of the best cures for a reluctant reader, after all, is a tale they cannot stop themselves from reading. And while we must tell our readers true things and give them weapons and give them armour and pass on whatever wisdom we have gleaned from our short stay on this green world, we have an obligation not to preach, not to lecture, not to force predigested morals and messages down our readers' throats like adult birds feeding their babies pre-masticated maggots; and we have an obligation never, ever, under any circumstances, to write anything for children that we would not want to read ourselves.

We have an obligation to understand and to acknowledge that as writers for children we are doing important work, because if we mess it up and write dull books that turn children away from reading and from books, we've lessened our own future and diminished theirs.

We all – adults and children, writers and readers – have an obligation to daydream. We have an obligation to imagine. It is easy to pretend that nobody can change anything, that we are in a world in which society is huge and the individual is less than nothing: an atom in a wall, a grain of rice in a rice field. But the truth is, individuals change their world over and over, individuals make the future, and they do it by imagining that things can be different.

Look around you: I mean it. Pause for a moment and look around the room that you are in. I'm going to point out something so obvious that it tends to be forgotten. It's this: that everything you can see, including the walls, was, at some point, imagined. Someone decided it was easier to sit on a chair than on the ground and imagined the chair. Someone had to imagine a way that I could talk to you in London right now without us all getting rained on. This room and the things in it, and all the other things in this building, this city, exist because, over and over and over, people imagined things.

We have an obligation to make things beautiful. Not to leave the world uglier than we found it, not to empty the oceans, not to leave our problems for the next generation. We have an obligation to clean up after ourselves, and not leave our children with a world we've shortsightedly messed up, shortchanged, and crippled.

We have an obligation to tell our politicians what we want, to vote against politicians of whatever party who do not understand the value of reading in creating worthwhile citizens, who do not want to act to preserve and protect knowledge and encourage literacy. This is not a matter of party politics. This is a matter of common humanity.

Albert Einstein was asked once how we could make our children intelligent. His reply was both simple and wise. "If you want your children to be intelligent," he said, "read them fairy tales. If you want them to be more intelligent, read them more fairy tales." He understood the value of reading, and of imagining. I hope we can give our children a world in which they will read, and be read to, and imagine, and understand.

Question 5 (5 marks)

State and explain **one** reason why you think this talk is or is not effective in arguing the importance of reading.

_____

_____

_____

_____

_____

_____

_____

Question 6 (10 marks)

Based on your reading of Neil Gaiman's talk, identify any **two** obligations that he suggests writers have to their readers. In your view, which **one** of these obligations is more important?

Optional Rough Work

EDCO SAMPLE A

_____
_____
_____
_____
_____
_____
_____
_____
_____
_____
_____
_____
_____

Question 7 (35 marks)

Parts (a) and (b) of this question are linked. Read both parts carefully before beginning your answer.

(a) *Fiction is the lie that tells the truth*.

Select a novel that you have studied for Junior Cycle English that you believe "tells the truth".
Give a reason for choosing this novel. (5 marks)

Title of novel: _____

Name of author: _____

```
                        Optional Rough Work




```

Reason for choosing the novel

_____

_____

_____

_____

(b) With reference to at least **two** key moments in your chosen novel, discuss how the novel
    tells the truth. (30 marks)

<table>
<tr><td>Optional Rough Work</td></tr>
</table>

_____

_____

_____

_____

_____

_____

_____

_____

_____

Suggested time for Section C: 20 minutes

Question 8   **(40 marks)**

The more we read poems the more we appreciate the skill and artistry of poets.

(a) With reference to a poem you have studied, explain where you believe the skill and artistry of the poet is most in evidence.

(b) Identify two poetic techniques that you believe require skill to use in an effective way. Give examples from the poetry you have studied that show the skill of the poet at work. (You may not use the poem discussed in (a) to answer this part of the question.)

Answer space for part (a)

Title of poem: _____

Name of poet: _____

Optional Rough Work

Answer space for part (b)

Poetic technique 1: _____

Poetic technique 2: _____

<table>
<tr><td>Optional Rough Work</td></tr>
</table>

_____
_____
_____
_____
_____
_____
_____
_____
_____
_____
_____
_____
_____
_____
_____
_____
_____

Suggested time for Section D: 20 minutes

In this edited extract from her book of letters written to aspiring writers, Maeve Binchy offers advice on writing a good story. Read the letter carefully and respond to the tasks that follow it.

Dear Writers' Club members,

1 I can't tell you what story to write. Nobody can do that except you. There is no point in telling anyone else what to write about. But I can share with you some of the advice I got along the way from wise editors, men and women who job it is to know what people like and to keep us writers somehow on the rails.

2 They say that when beginning a story you should always try to catch people at some interesting juncture in their lives, like when they have to make a choice or decision, or when someone has betrayed them, or the start of love or the end of love. It's better to come across them at some kind of crisis than in the middle of a long, lazy summer where nothing happens.

3 The notion of change is important in a story. It would be a dull tale indeed if the hero took no notice of the disintegration of his family, if he was the same unaltered dullard after four hundred pages. The reader would feel fairly short changed.

4 They told me that we must be interested in the hero or heroine – that doesn't mean making the person into a walking saint or goody-goody, but it does mean giving them a strong and memorable personality. There is no point whatsoever in spending pages and pages describing someone who is a dithering, dull kind of person without purpose, views or motivation. We have to care enough about the people to follow them through to the last page. When I heard this I began to panic a bit and asked humbly what kind of person might be interesting enough to hold the reader's attention. I wouldn't be able to create Captain Ahab, the man who pursued Moby Dick, or Rhett Butler who didn't give a damn in *Gone with the Wind*. But I was told that writing wasn't a matter of painting by numbers. They couldn't just create some formula leaving me to join up the dots. I had to think, and work out the kind of people whose lives and adventures I would be interested in myself. This way I might be on the way to make others interested in them too.

5 In my case I was interested in people who were told that if they were good they would be happy, and therefore disappointed when it didn't always turn out like that. So I worked out that, in a way, people create their own happiness not just by being good, whatever that is, but by seeking opportunities, taking chances, taking charge of their own destiny. It interested me for a start, and then kept me going. It could work for you too, if you found a theory around which to base a story.

6 Another good piece of advice I got was to think of the story as a journey. Something happens to the main character at the start, and we follow him or her dealing with it, or not dealing with it, or ignoring it, or making it worse. Whatever. Now I don't mean a literal journey, they don't even have to leave home. But they have to progress, be different people for better or worse at the end. The man who thinks his son is on hard drugs, his colleagues in the office on the take or his own gambling out of control, has to do something. You can't leave him static in the same plight at the end of chapter fourteen as he was at the outset. The woman who has had a bad medical diagnosis, a faithless friend, an unjust accusation of shoplifting or proof that her brother is a murderer must have taken steps of some sort over whatever it is. She can't just sit there page after page letting it all wash over her.

7 They also say that pace is important when you are telling a story. Again, nobody can hold your hand over this, but I have found that at the beginning it helps to make a kind of chart of the book chapter by chapter, giving yourself orders like, "By the end of chapter two we must know that she cannot afford to pay the rent and will be evicted", and then "By the end of chapter three we must know that her rent will be paid for her, but at a price." If you do this in advance it stops you dawdling about till you're ready and generally dragging the thing out and making it endless. There is no right or wrong pace, it's up to you. A gentle lyrical story will call for one kind of speed, a fast-moving thriller another. But there's no harm being aware of it.

8 I hope it's all going well for you and that you are getting your ten pages a week done.

Question 9   **(15 marks)**

Do you find Maeve Binchy's advice helpful or entertaining? Explain your answer with reference to the text. You may refer to the letter's content and/or its style.

Optional Rough Work

Question 10 (25 marks)

Having read Maeve Binchy's article, write a letter to young writers who subscribe to a website for aspiring writers. Your letter should contain your advice on writing a memorable story.

Junior Cycle 20XX
Final Examination Sample B

English

Higher Level

Day Date June – Morning 9:30 to 11:30

180 marks

Examination number

The theme of this examination paper is
Communication

Instructions

There are **four** sections in this examination paper.

Section A	Reading to Analyse and Evaluate	35 marks	2 questions
Section B	Appreciating Story	45 marks	2 questions
Section C	Appreciating Language, Character, Relationships and Stage Craft	75 marks	5 questions
Section D	Writing to Engage with Your Audience	25 marks	1 question

Answer all 10 questions.

The questions do not all carry equal marks. The number of marks for each question is stated at the top of the question.

You should spend about 25 minutes on Section A.
You should spend about 30 minutes on Section B and about 45 minutes on Section C.
You should spend about 15 minutes on Section D.

When answering on studied material, you must use texts prescribed for examination in 20XX.

Write your answers in the spaces provided in this booklet. You may lose marks if you do not do so. Space is provided for extra work. Label any extra work clearly with the question number and part.

You may only use blue or black pen when writing your answers. Do not use pencil.

The examination booklet will be scanned and your work will be presented to an examiner on screen. Anything that you write outside of the answer areas may not be seen by the examiner.

Read the following passage. It is taken from a radio interview given by Sherry Turkle to the radio presenter Terry Gross. The theme of the interview is the effect of digital devices on communication. The passage is written to reflect the way the interview was given before a live audience. Answer the questions which follow.

GROSS: Sherry Turkle, welcome. One of the things you write about in your new book, *Alone Together*, is how children have grown up in a culture of distraction.

TURKLE: Yes.

GROSS: I assumed there that you would be talking about how children and teens are so distracted by texting their friends all the time, but you're talking about children's parents, too ...

TURKLE: Yes.

GROSS: ... that children's parents are distracted. I want you to describe some of the complaints that children have expressed to you about their parents being distracted by their personal devices.

TURKLE: Yeah, well, what my fieldwork has shown is that from the minute these children met this technology, it was the competition. I do my fieldwork in playgrounds, and parents are texting and on cell phones as their kids play on the jungle gyms and swings, and parents text during breakfast and dinner as their children beg them for attention.

Parents text at games when the kids are on the playing field, often missing the big score. Parents are on the phone in cars, and the kids are left to text in the backseat on their devices instead of having those precious moments, you know, to find out what – to eavesdrop on your kids or talk to your kids in the car on the way to school.

So children grow up learning that they're not the centre of their parents' attention. One of the most poignant interviews I did was with a young man who talked about how his father used to watch the Sunday games with him and maybe have the Sunday newspaper between them and share the sports section or the news section.

And now his father does his email and texts. And it's just not the same. He misses his dad.

GROSS: So let's turn the tables. What are some of the complaints that parents shared with you about their children being distracted by their cell phones and other devices?

TURKLE: Well, parents then suffer the slings and arrows of not having their children's attention, and I think that what's the big change I see now is that parents are starting to accept, really over the past two years, a little bit of the responsibility for that. It's hard to get your child's attention because your child doesn't want, for example, to answer your calls. Your child will only respond to a text message.

EDCO SAMPLE B

This is a very common complaint of parents. Children during dinner will want to text. It's very hard to get them to come to dinner and eat, and so what I suggest to parents is that they use dinners as really sacred spaces where they say look, dinner is a time when we come together as a family, and if I haven't followed these rules since you were young, I'm sorry. I've made mistakes, too, but now we're starting to put a basket, you know, in the kitchen and in the dining room, and we all put our phones in that basket, and we...

GROSS: Are they turned off?

(LAUGHTER)

TURKLE: And the phones are turned off just as a lot of professors are starting to say, you know, look, we've taken things too far, and we put a basket in the classroom, and this seminar really is for us having a conversation together. Because we know that our ...

GROSS: Do you do that?

TURKLE: I'm starting to, because I taught a course last semester, and halfway through the course – it was a course on memoir, a course in which the students in the course were sharing very really intimate details of their life. It's a course where students talk about their lives.

           We read memoirs, and then the students write memoirs, and members of the class admitted that they were texting, kind of, under the desks. And we talked about it in class, and it was not OK that there was texting during class, and we just decided that ...

GROSS: And your objection to that was that people were sharing intimate moments, and other people weren't paying attention? Or were you afraid somebody was, like, live tweeting somebody's personal confessions?

TURKLE: No, the objection of the class was that this was really a conversation and that we were losing – that we were losing the sense of this class as a conversation, and that that is the value of what we're there to do together is to have a conversation together and that that is what we should be about.

           And what the students thought – we had a great conversation about what was so seductive about texting, and essentially I heard from the students what I hear from so many adults. I think we've over-hyped the difference between students – between young people and older people on this issue.

           And they all say to me that what's so seductive about texting, about keeping that phone on, about that little red light on the BlackBerry, is you want to know who wants you.

'Fresh Air' with Terry Gross is produced at WHYY is Philadelphia and distributed by NPR. Podcasts are avilable at www.npr.org/podcasts and at iTunes.

Question 1 (15 marks)

Name one consequence that Sherry Turkle suggests arises from parents and children not giving each other their full attention.

_____

_____

_____

_____

_____

_____

_____

_____

_____

_____

Question 2 (20 marks)

Suggest two ways that Sherry Turkle makes her answers interesting for the listeners. You can refer to what she says or her way of saying it.

```
Optional Rough Work




```

_____

_____

_____

_____

_____

_____

_____

_____

_____

Additional Writing Space. Label all work clearly with the question number and part.

Question 3   **(20 marks)**

Give the title and author of a novel you have studied on your course.

Title: _____

Author: _____

How did the text communicate to you that the central character had developed over the course of the novel?

_____

_____

_____

_____

_____

_____

_____

_____

_____

_____

_____

_____

_____

_____

_____

_____

_____

_____

_____

_____

_____

_____

Question 4 (25 marks)

In your view, which of the following was the most important in adding to your enjoyment of the novel:
  – The setting of the story
  – The action of the story
  – The writer's style and use of language

Explain your answer as clearly as possible.

_____

_____

_____

_____

_____

_____

_____

_____

_____

_____

_____

_____

_____

_____

_____

_____

_____

_____

_____

_____

_____

Additional Writing Space. Label all work clearly with the question number and part.

Read this scene from Shakespeare's play *Henry IV*, Part I.

England is on the verge of civil war. Harry Percy (known as Hotspur) is one of a group of conspirators who are plotting against King Henry. Fearing that the plot will be betrayed, Hotspur decides to act without delay. Hotspur's wife, Kate (Lady Percy), concerned by her husband's recent behaviour, asks for an explanation.

Enter Hotspur, reading a letter from a lord who refuses to join forces with him against the King.

Hotspur: (Reading the letter) "The purpose you undertake is dangerous, the friends you have named uncertain, the time itself unsorted, and your whole plot too light for the counterpoise of so great an opposition."

Say you so, say you so? I say unto you again, you are a shallow, cowardly hind, and you lie. Our plot is a good plot as ever was laid, and our friends true and constant. If I were now by this rascal I could brain him with his lady's fan. Is there not my father, my uncle and myself? Lord Edmund Mortimer, my Lord of York and Owen Glendower? Have I not all their letters to meet me in arms by the ninth of the next month? What a pagan rascal is this? Ha! Will he to the King; and lay open all our proceedings! Hang him, let him tell the King: we are prepared! I will set forward tonight.
(Enter Lady Kate Percy)
How now, Kate? I must leave you within these two hours.

Kate: O my good lord, why are you thus alone?
Tell me, sweet lord, what is it that takes from thee thy golden sleep?
Why hast thou lost the fresh blood in thy cheeks;
And given my treasures and my rights of thee
To thick-eyed musing and cursed melancholy?
In thy faint slumbers I by thee have watched,
And heard thee murmur tales of iron wars,
Cry, *Courage! To the field!*
Thy spirit within thee hath been so at war,
And thus hath so bestirred thee in thy sleep,
That beads of sweat have stood upon thy brow,
Like bubbles in a late-disturbed stream.
Some heavy business hath my lord in hand,
And I must know it, else he loves me not.
(Enter a Servant)

Hotspur: What ho! Hath Butler brought those horses?

Servant: One horse, my lord, he brought it even now.

Hotspur: What horse? A roan*, a crop-ear, is it not?   (*A horse's coat colour)

Servant: It is my lord.

Hotspur: That roan shall be my throne. Well, I will back him straight.
(Exit Servant)

Kate: But hear you my lord.

Hotspur: What say'st thou, my lady?

Kate: What is it carries you away?

Hotspur: Why, my horse, my love, my horse.

Kate: Out, you mad-headed ape! I'll know your business, Harry, that I will.
Answer my directly unto this question that I ask.

Hotspur: Away! Away, you trifler! Love! I love thee not. I care not for thee Kate.
This is no world to play with mammets*, and to tilt with lips.   (*Dolls)
We must have bloody noses and cracked crowns.

Kate: Do you not love me? Do you not indeed?
Well do not then; for since you love me not,
I will not love myself. Do you not love me?
Nay, tell me if you speak in jest or no?

Hotspur: When I am on horseback, I will swear I love thee infinitely.
But hark you, Kate, I must not have you henceforth question me
Whither I go, nor reason whereabout:
Whither I must, I must. This evening must I leave you, gentle Kate.
But hark you, Kate, whither I go, thither shall you go too.
Today will I set forth, tomorrow you.
Will this content you, Kate?

Kate: It must, of force.   (Exeunt)

Question 5   **(15 marks)**

Explain, in your own words, the meaning of the following quotations from the text.

(a) *Lay open all our proceedings*

Meaning: _____

_____

(b) *What is it that takes from thee thy golden sleep?*

Meaning: _____

_____

(c) *Why hast thou lost the fresh blood in thy cheeks?*

Meaning: _____

_____

(d) *Some heavy business hath my lord in hand*

Meaning: _____

_____

(e) *I'll know your business*:

Meaning: _____

_____

Question 6   **(15 marks)**

Based on your reading of the scene, do you think that Hotspur and Kate have a good relationship?
Refer to the text to support your answer.

_____

_____

_____

_____

_____

_____

_____

_____

_____

Question 7 (15 marks)

You are playing the part of either Kate or Hotspur. Describe **three** things you would do to convey your feelings and state of mind to the audience.

_____

_____

_____

_____

_____

_____

_____

_____

_____

_____

Question 8 (15 marks)

Choose a scene from a Shakespearean play you have studied which reveals something important about the way two characters communicate with each other.

Title of Play:

_____

Name of Character 1:

_____

Name of Character 2:

_____

(a) Describe the situation and the nature of the communication between the two characters.

_____

_____

_____

_____

_____

_____

(b) Which of the characters did you find most engaging? Explain your answer.

_____

_____

_____

_____

_____

_____

_____

_____

_____

Question 9   **(15 marks)**

Four hundred years after his death, Shakespeare's plays are as popular as ever. Based on a Shakespearean play you have studied, suggest three reasons for Shakespeare's enduring popularity.

Question 10   **(25 marks)**

Study the script below and complete the task which follows.

Using one or more of the scenarios described in the script, write the voiceover for a new radio drama in which a young person described how he or she has developed superpowers.

You may take a serious or a humorous approach in your text.

You may refer to location and the use of sound effects in your script.

_____

_____

_____

_____

Additional Writing Space. Label all work clearly with the question number and part.

Junior Cycle 20XX
Final Examination Sample C

English

Higher Level

Day Date June – Morning 9:30 to 11:30

180 marks

The theme of this examination paper is
Family Adventures

Instructions

There are **three** sections in this examination paper.

Section A	Understanding Characters	65 marks	3 questions
Section B	Responding to Texts	60 marks	2 questions
Section C	Reading and Writing with Competence	55 marks	4 questions

Answer all 9 questions.

The questions do not all carry equal marks. The number of marks for each question is stated at the top of the question.

You should spend about 40 minutes on Section A, 40 minutes on Section B and 35 minutes on Section C.

When answering on studied material, you must use texts in line with what is prescribed for 201X.

Write your answers in the spaces provided in this booklet. You may lose marks if you do not do so.

You are not required to use all of the space provided. You should read each question in full before beginning your response.

Extra pages are provided if needed. Label any extra work clearly with the question number and part.

You may only use blue or black pen when writing your answers. Do not use pencil.

The examination booklet will be scanned and your work will be presented to an examiner on screen. Anything that you write outside of the answer areas may not be seen by the examiner.

Read this scene from the stage adaptation of Michael Morpurgo's novel, *Kensuke's Kingdom*, and answer the questions which follow.

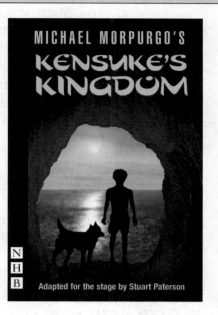

Michael, his mother, and the family dog, Stella, have arrived at a repair shed where Michael's father has a surprise for them.

FATHER: There's someone I want you to meet. She's called Peggy Sue. She'd been looking forward to meeting you… I've told her about you…

He pulls away the sheets to reveal a gleaming boat with the name 'Peggy Sue' painted on it. Michael and his mother stare in amazement.

FATHER: So there you are … what do you think?

MOTHER: (*Utterly stunned*) She's a yacht!

MICHAEL: She's fantastic!

FATHER: I've had her checked. She's a Bowman. Best make, best design there is, and the safest …

MOTHER: (*Still unable to take it in*) She's a yacht!

FATHER: You know what I couldn't take? After the factory closed the only wage coming into our house was Michael's paper round.

MICHAEL: I didn't mind …

FATHER: I know you didn't, but I did. It drove me mad, so I started to think …
What's always been the most special thing for us?
Sailing our dinghy on Sundays, right?
All three of us, and Stella, on the reservoir.
And then I thought, why not make our whole life special, not just Sundays?
We've got redundancy money, there's a bit saved, the money I got from the car …
I know, we could do what everyone else does and put it in the bank, but what for?
Just to watch it dribble away until there's nothing left?
Or we could do something really special with it, a once-in-a-lifetime thing.
We could sail around the world. Africa, South America, Australia, the Pacific.
We could see places we've only dreamed of.

MOTHER: Around the world?

FATHER: I know – you're thinking we've only sailed a dinghy, he's gone crazy, it's too dangerous, we'll be flat broke …

MOTHER: I'm not leaving my home. I was born there. I'm not leaving.

FATHER: It wouldn't be for ever … a year, maybe eighteen months!
And we'll train before we go … learn to be proper sailors.
You, Mum, you'll do your Yachmaster's certificate. Oh, didn't I say?
You'd be skipper, Mum. I'll be first mate and handyman.
Michael, you'll be cabin boy …
And Stella – I know it's a terrible insults – but you'll have to be ship's cat.
A few month's training and we'll be off round the world.
Linda, the world! What do you think?

MICHAEL: Fan-tas-tic!

But his mother has not given her reply.

FATHER: It'll be the adventure of a lifetime. It's our chance, Linda. We'll never get
another. What do you say?

MOTHER: (*after a pause*) I'll be skipper you say?

FATHER & MICHAEL: (*in unison*) Aye, aye, cap'n!

Question 1 **(20 marks)**

(a) Father has most to say in the scene. Based on what he says, what kind of person is he? (10)

_____

_____

_____

_____

_____

_____

_____

(b) You are the director of the play. Write a brief note describing how you would instruct the actor taking the part of Father to play his part. (10)

Optional Rough Work

Note for Actor Playing Father

_____

_____

_____

_____

_____

_____

_____

_____

Question 2   **(40 marks)**

Choose a play you have studied in which a character makes an important decision. Describe the circumstances in which the decision is made. To what extent was your sympathy for and understanding of the character deepened by this decision?

Title of the play _____

Name of the character _____

_____

_____

_____

_____

_____

_____

_____

_____

_____

_____

_____

_____

_____

_____

_____

_____

_____

_____

_____

_____

_____

_____

_____

Question 3   **(5 marks)**

In the case of each of the following words indicate what the word means by placing a tick ✓ beside the appropriate box.

(a) aside

☐ A short speech spoken by a character in a play

☐ Part of the action that takes place off stage

(b) auditorium

☐ The box in the theatre which houses the sound equipment

☐ The part of theatre where the audience sits

(c) dialogue

☐ Words spoken between characters in a play

☐ The speech made before the action of the play begins

(d) narrator

☐ The person who tells the story of the play

☐ The person who directs the play

(e) stage directions

☐ Instructions telling actors how they are to move or speak their lines

☐ Direction for the audience entering and exiting a theatre

Question 4   **(45 marks)**

(a) Choose any two poems from your course which dealt with families. Give the title and author of each poem. (Marks are awarded for accuracy and spelling.)

Poem 1   Poem 2

Title: _____   Title: _____

Author: _____   Author: _____

Which poem appealed to you most? In answering you must refer to at least two of the following: Treatment of Theme; Use of Language; Memorable Images; Voice and Tone.   (30)

```
┌─────────────────────────────────────────────────────────────┐
│                     Optional Rough Work                       │
│                                                               │
│                                                               │
│                                                               │
│                                                               │
│                                                               │
│                                                               │
│                                                               │
│                                                               │
│                                                               │
└─────────────────────────────────────────────────────────────┘
```

_____

_____

_____

_____

_____

_____

_____

_____

_____

_____

_____

_____

_____

_____

_____

_____

_____

_____

_____

_____

_____

_____

_____

_____

_____

_____

_____

_____

(b) Imagine you are going to write a poem on the theme of families. What feeling would you
    like to convey in your poem and suggest how you would do this.   (15)

_____

_____

_____

_____

_____

_____

_____

_____

_____

_____

_____

_____

Read the following poem by Linda Pastan and answer the question which follow.

To A Daughter Leaving Home

When I taught you
at eight to ride
a bicycle, loping along
beside you
as you wobbled away
on two round wheels,
my own mouth rounding
in surprise when you pulled
ahead down the curved
path of the park,
I kept waiting
for the thud
of your crash as I
sprinted to catch up,
while you grew
smaller, more breakable
with distance,
pumping, pumping
for your life, screaming
with laughter,
the hair flapping
behind you like a
handkerchief waving
goodbye.

Linda Pastan

Question 5   **(15 marks)**

What aspects of the poem *To a Daughter Leaving Home* are particularly effective? Explain your answer with reference to the poem.

_____

_____

_____

_____

_____

_____

_____

_____

_____

_____

Read the following text by Nell McCafferty. Answer the questions which follow.

They didn't come to plead. They came to hustle, and they knew exactly what they wanted. The door of the Children's Court opened and they trotted in, making a busy beeline straight for the Justice's bench. They leaned confidentially over the wooden top, three heads as one, and started chattering to her. An overnight stay in custody in a Garda station had not improved their appearance. Those three little faces had not seen water in days. Jimmy, in the middle, and the smallest, was the star. His small bum, clad brightly in blue and white striped underpants, protruded unabashed through a gaping split in his wine-coloured trousers. The ladies' shoes, outsize, which he wore, clattered cheerily as he tried to move his feet. His hair was an old-fashioned crew-cut, but thick. 'Me mother's sick,' he gazed up at the Justice. 'In fact,' said the guard, 'he has left his mother, since the father left, and he stays with this other boy. His parents wouldn't come to court, either.'

'Now boys,' said the bemused Justice, 'did you break and enter such and such a house?' 'Yes,' chorused her class of three. 'And did you break and enter such and such another house?' 'Yes,' they said delightedly.

'We'd like to go to St Laurence's for three months, to keep us out of trouble,' said Jimmy, hoisting himself up onto the bench with his elbow, leaving his shoes behind.

'Wait a minute,' said the Justice. 'Did you enter this other house?' 'Yes,' they said, 'and we'd like to go to St. Laurence's.'

'Aren't you the terrible little divils? Aren't you now?' asked the Justice, smiling, as she abandoned all pretence of legal mien. They grinned.

Finally, they had broken into the Jesuit college and stolen cash from the phone booth and mission box, and had been caught in the act.

The parents of Jimmy's friend would not come to court, the guard said, because, they said, the guards were with them every week about the boy, and they wanted him sent to St. Laurence's.

'Yes, St. Laurence's, for three months,' they squealed excitedly.

'Why three months?' asked the Justice.

'We'd like to be out for Christmas,' explained Jimmy.

'I don't think St Laurence's will be very glad to receive the three of you,' said the Justice. 'I'll send you up there until this day week, till we see what we're going to do with you.'

'Thanks, thanks,' they squealed, and they ran back to the door, nudging each other gleefully.

'We're going, we're going,' Jimmy joyfully announced to the people outside.

'God save us and bless us,' said the Justice to the registrar.

Question 6   (15 marks)

Based on your reading of this article:

- Explain in your own words what happened in the court.
- Did the judge impress you in the way she handled the case? Give reasons for your answer.

_____

_____

_____

_____

_____

_____

_____

_____

_____

_____

_____

_____

_____

Question 7 (5 marks)

The following words, in bold, appear in the above passage. In the case of each word or phrase, indicate what it means, as it is used in the passage, by placing a tick ✓ in the appropriate box. Tick one box only in each case.

(a) Confidentially

trustingly ☐ secretively ☐ boldly ☐

(b) In custody

in the ownership of ☐ in the care and control of ☐ in the possession of ☐

(c) Unabashed

unashamed ☐ unseen ☐ apologetic ☐

(d) Bemused

confused ☐ clear-headed ☐ strict ☐

(e) Pretence

appearance ☐ effort ☐ seriousness ☐

Question 8 (15 marks)

Do you think the writer of this article uses language effectively to convey the atmosphere of the court to the reader? Explain your answer with reference to the article.

_____

_____

_____

_____

_____

_____

_____

_____

_____

_____

_____
_____
_____
_____
_____
_____
_____
_____
_____
_____
_____
_____
_____
_____

Question 9 **(20 marks)**

'Aren't you the terrible little divils? Aren't you now?' asked the Justice, smiling...

You are participating in a debate on the motion that: *'Children who break the law should be treated leniently by the courts.'* You must either agree or disagree with the motion.

State and develop any two points you would make to persuade an audience attending the debate that your views deserve to be supported.

_____
_____
_____
_____
_____
_____
_____
_____

Junior Cycle 20XX
Final Examination Sample D

English

Higher Level

Day Date June – Morning 9:30 to 11:30

180 marks

Examination number

The theme of this examination paper is
Exile

Instructions

There are **three** sections in this examination paper.

Section A	Appreciating Ideas, Arguments and Tone	65 marks	4 questions
Section B	Analysing and Responding	35 marks	4 questions
Section C	Writing for a Variety of Purposes	80 marks	2 questions

Answer all 10 questions.

The questions do not all carry equal marks. The number of marks for each question is stated at the top of the question.

You should spend about 40 minutes on Section A.
You should spend about 20 minutes on Section B.
You should spend about 50 minutes on Section C.

Write your answers in the spaces provided in this booklet. You may lose marks if you do not do so. Space is provided for extra work. Label any extra work clearly with the question number and part.

You may only use blue or black pen when writing your answers. Do not use pencil.

The examination booklet will be scanned and your work will be presented to an examiner on screen. Anything that you write outside of the answer areas may not be seen by the examiner.

Section A   Appreciating Ideas, Arguments and Tone

In this extract from his speech to members of the European Parliament, António Guterres, the UN High Commissioner for Refugees, gives his views on the refugee crisis and Europe's response to it. Read the extract and answer the questions which follow.

Ladies and Gentlemen,

Dear colleagues,

Today, unfortunately, we may have a European Union, but Europe is no longer united; Europe is divided (…) It is as if each country in Europe was a piece of a puzzle, but when you put the pieces together you discover that they do not match anymore. There is no such space as a Europe acting together to grant protection to those in need, and this is causing enormous suffering to people. In interviews at the different borders, especially with Syrians, we see an enormous perplexity, uncertainty, people do not know what is going to happen; many feel fear, and some despair (…)

Now, why this spike all of a sudden? Of course last year there was a big growth in arrivals in the central Mediterranean. This year they are more or less at the same level, but this is a trend that will grow with the demographics of Africa and Europe. But the sudden spike within this growing trend, in my interpretation, is for a combination of three reasons. First, we have now had Syrians in the neighbouring countries for nearly five years. They have lost hope in a political solution in Syria. Second, the living conditions in the neighbouring countries have been dramatically deteriorating. We have to acknowledge that this huge population increase in countries like Jordan or Lebanon, even in Turkey to some extent, has a dramatic impact in the economies and societies and is causing big problems in these countries. And in this situation, refugees are not allowed to work, have no form to organize their lives, and as savings disappear, the living conditions deteriorate more and more and more, and hope tends to disappear as well. To make things worse, in 2015 we have witnessed a decrease in international assistance. The key element in this decrease was the lack of funding for World Food Programme, which had to implement a few months ago a cut in food assistance by about 40% in the neighbouring countries. And that gave people the impression that they were going to be abandoned. You can imagine – no hope to go back, living conditions getting worse and worse in the countries that have made enormous efforts to receive refugees but that have no capacity to provide for them, and now the feeling that the international community is forgetting about them with new crises starting elsewhere. In this situation Europe appeared as the only salvation, and you know how social media work, and how smugglers immediately enter into action, and so this started to grow and gain the dimension we have witnessed in the recent past.

In this context, it is clear for me that massive humanitarian support to the refugees, and massive structural and economic support to the neighbouring countries are absolute preconditions to allow for this flow to be contained.

I would also like to underline what was said by my good friend Federica Mogherini: we need to combine a much more effective combatting of smuggling and trafficking with a much bigger offer of legal ways for people to enter Europe. That includes resettlement, and I am glad that the resettlement project was approved. It also includes humanitarian admission, family reunification, visas that can be given for all kinds of reasons. To do this would mean that we do not only provide reception and relocation for the people that arrive by boat, but one of our objectives should also be to reduce as much as possible the number of people forced to take these tragic routes in which so many perish and in which so many are exploited in horrible situations.

But let me end with what was also said by Federica Mogherini: this looks unmanageable, but it is perfectly manageable. But for something to be manageable, you have to manage it. And that means you need to have the reception, the relocation and all the instruments in place and working effectively.

4,000 people per day in the Greek islands is of course a big flow. But the number of people displaced by conflict in the world per day last year was 42,500. We now have one third of the population in Lebanon that is Palestinian and Syrian; Syrians are one fourth of the population. If one looks at other situations in Africa and in other parts of the world, we see extremely poor countries that open their borders and provide what they have – and even what they do not have – to support people. I will never forget, when the Côte d'Ivoire crisis erupted, I went to Liberia to a refugee hosting village. And before any international assistance had arrived, the people of that Liberian village were giving the refugees coming from Côte d'Ivoire the seeds of rice that they were going to use for the next planting season. They were condemning themselves to starve, unless international support would be given, just to allow for the refugees to survive. This kind of example from very poor people is something that the European Union should meditate on – with all the economic problems and difficulties and all the crises, by which my own country was also deeply affected, we still live in a privileged part of the world. And we have an enormous responsibility when we look around and see what is happening today around Europe, knowing that sooner or later, if we do not do the right thing, we will pay a heavy price.

Thank you.

Question 1 (5 marks)

According to UN Commissioner António Guterres, is Europe united in dealing with the refugee crisis? Explain your answer.

_____

_____

_____

_____

_____

Question 2   **(35 marks)**

(a) The UN Commissioner António Guterres suggests three reasons for the increase in refugees. What are they?

Reason 1: _____

_____

_____

_____

_____

Reason 2: _____

_____

_____

_____

_____

Reason 3: _____

_____

_____

_____

(b) Which of these explanations do you find most convincing. Explain your choice.

_____

_____

_____

_____

_____

_____

_____

_____

_____

_____

(c) Do you think that António Guterres is sympathetic to the plight of the refugees? Explain your answer.

_____

_____

_____

_____

_____

_____

_____

_____

_____

_____

Question 3   **(15 marks)**

Choose three examples of words or phrases used in the speech which you think would influence the attitude of the listeners to the plight of the refugees. Explain your choices.

Example 1: _____

_____

Reason for Choosing: _____

_____

_____

_____

_____

Example 2: _____

_____

Reason for Choosing: _____

_____

_____

_____

_____

Example 3: _____

Reason for Choosing: _____

_____

_____

_____

_____

Question 4   (10 marks)

Identify any two elements in this text which identify it as a spoken rather than a written text.
Explain your choices.

Element 1: _____

_____

_____

_____

_____

Element 2: _____

_____

_____

_____

_____

Ireland's Refugee Plan

What do we know so far?

Who will arrive?

Refugees from Syria and Eritrea - mostly from those groups already in Greece and Hungary.

How will claims be assessed?

European Commission system in Greece, Hungary and Italy for preliminary assessments. Then further assessment and security checks in Ireland.

Task force set up to manage programme

Including people from government departments, voluntary organisations and the religious community.

What is the plan for welcoming refugees?

There will be emergency reception and orientation centres around the country

Where will the refugees live?

Dept of defence & OPW properties will be audited for suitability for initial accommodation.

Direct Provision?

No.

The Govt expects 90% of refugee status applications to be successful and for refugees to be able to work soon after arrival.

Integration?

English language education will be a priority for people arriving with no English language skills, to aid integration

The Cost?

€12m per 1000 refugees – €12,000 per refugee (Govt estimates)

European aid?

The European Commission will provide €6,000 per refugee

Study the info-graphic on Ireland's refugee plan and then answer the questions which follow, using the information provided in the document.

(a) The refugees who will arrive in Ireland will come from _____ and

_____.

(b) Name the three countries where preliminary assessments of refugees will occur:

Country A _____

Country B _____

Country C _____

(c) Apart from government departments, name two groups who will be represented on the task force to manage the refugee plan: _____ and

_____.

(d) What is the estimated cost of the plan per refugee? _____

(e) What percentage of this cost will be provided by the European Commission? _____

(f) What initiative will be taken to help with integration of refugees?

_____

_____

(g) Where will refugees live when they first come to Ireland?

_____

_____

Question 6 (5 marks)

In the context of a policy on refugees, what do you think is the meaning of the phrase 'direct provision'?

_____

_____

_____

_____

_____

Question 7   (15 marks)

You have been told that three refugee families, consisting of parents, children and grandchildren, will be located in your community. Suggest three initiatives that you think would help the families settle into their new lives. Explain your thinking.

Optional Rough Work

Initiative 1: _____

_____

_____

_____

_____

Initiative 2: _____

_____

_____

_____

_____

Initiative 3: _____

_____

_____

_____

Question 8   (5 marks)

Your school launches a 'Welcome Campaign' for five new students who come from refugee families.

Write a slogan for the campaign.

_____

_____

Additional Writing Space. Label all work clearly with the question number and part.

_____

_____

_____

_____

_____

_____

_____

_____

_____

_____

_____

_____

_____

_____

Read the following poems by W. B. Yeats and Patrick Kavanagh on the theme of exile and complete the tasks which follow.

Kerr's Ass

We borrowed the loan of Kerr's big ass
To go to Dundalk with butter,
Brought him home the evening before the market
An exile that night in Mucker.

We heeled up the cart before the door,
We took the harness inside
The straw-stuffed straddle, the broken breeching
With bits of bull-wire tied;

The winkers that had no choke-band,
The collar and the reins ...
In Ealing Broadway, London Town
I name their several names

Until a world comes to life –
Morning, the silent bog,
And the God of imagination waking
In a Mucker fog.

Patrick Kavanagh

The Lake Isle of Innisfree

I will arise and go now, and go to Innisfree,
And a small cabin build there, of clay and wattles made;
Nine bean-rows will I have there, a hive for the honey-bee,
And live alone in the bee-loud glade.

And I shall have some peace there, for peace comes dropping slow,
Dropping from the veils of the morning to where the cricket sings;
There midnight's all a glimmer, and noon a purple glow,
And evening full of the linnet's wings.

I will arise and go now, for always night and day
I hear lake water lapping with low sounds by the shore;
While I stand on the roadway, or on the pavements grey,
I hear it in the deep heart's core.

William Butler Yeats

Question 9   (50 marks)

(a) In your view which poem is most effective in portraying the feelings of an exile?

Kerr's Ass

The Lake Isle of Innisfree

(b) Your class has read both poems. Write the script of a speech you would make to persuade your fellow students that the poem you have chosen is the most effective in portraying the feelings of an exile. Your speech piece should analyse the poem using appropriate vocabulary and persuade your audience of the merits of your case.

Optional Rough Work

Question 10   **(30 marks)**

Based on a real or an imagined experience, write a reflective piece on being far from home. Your piece should:

- Describe where you are

- Capture the emotions you experience

- Express your thoughts about home

You may choose a suitable form, such as an essay, an email, a blog or a diary.

Optional Rough Work

Additional Writing Space. Label all work clearly with the question number and part.

Junior Cycle 20XX
Final Examination Sample E

English

Higher Level

Day Date June – Morning 9:30 to 11:30

180 marks

Examination number

The theme of this examination paper is
Education for All

Instructions

There are **three** sections in this examination paper.

Section A	Reading to Understand	80 marks	6 questions
Section B	Responding Imaginatively	75 marks	4 questions
Section C	Reading Comprehension	25 marks	2 questions

Answer all 12 questions.

The questions do not all carry equal marks. The number of marks for each question is stated at the top of the question.

You should spend about 50 minutes on Section A.
You should spend about 45 minutes on Section B.
You should spend about 15 minutes on Section C.

When answering on studied material, you must refer to texts prescribed for examination in 20XX.

Write your answers in the spaces provided in this booklet. You may lose marks if you do not do so. Space is provided for extra work. Label any extra work clearly with the question number and part.

You may only use blue or black pen when writing your answers. Do not use pencil.

The examination booklet will be scanned and your work will be presented to an examiner on screen. Anything that you write outside of the answer areas may not be seen by the examiner.

Section A Reading to Understand – Campaigning for Education

Read this edited extract from Malala Yousafzai's autobiography and then answer the questions which follow.

This text is based on extracts from Pakistani teenager Malala Yousafzai's book *I Am Malala*, co-written with journalist Christina Lamb. Malala campaigned for education for girls in her community and as a result she was shot and badly injured. In this passage, we learn about Malala's new life in England, her old life in Pakistan and that terrible attack.

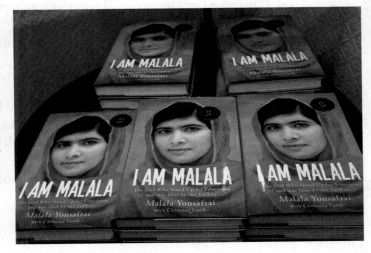

1. One year ago I left my home for school and never returned. I was shot by a Taliban bullet and was flown out of Pakistan unconscious … Now, every morning when I open my eyes, I long to see my old room full of my things, my clothes all over the floor and my school prizes on the shelves. Instead I am in a country [England] which is five hours behind my beloved homeland … But my country is centuries behind this one.

2. Here there is any convenience you can imagine. Water running from every tap, hot or cold as you wish; lights at the flick of a switch, day and night, no need for oil lamps; ovens to cook on that don't need anyone to go and fetch gas cylinders from the bazaar. Here everything is so modern one can even find food ready cooked in packets. When I stand in front of my window and look out, I see tall buildings, long roads full of vehicles moving in orderly lines, neat green hedges and lawns and tidy pavements to walk on. I close my eyes and for a moment I am back in my valley – the high snow-topped mountains, green waving fields and fresh blue rivers – and my heart smiles …

3. … I had been given … an award for campaigning for peace in our valley and the right for girls to go to school. On some shelves were all the gold-coloured plastic trophies I had won for coming first in my class. Only twice had I not come top – both times when I was beaten by my class rival Malka e-Noor. I was determined that would not happen again … I told my best friend Moniba everything. We'd lived on the same street … and had been friends since primary school and we shared everything, Justin Bieber songs and *Twilight* movies, the best face-lightening creams. Her dream was to be a fashion designer although she knew her family would never agree to it, so she told everyone she wanted to be a doctor. It's hard for girls in our society to be anything other than teachers or doctors, if they can work at all. I was different – I never hid my desire … to be an inventor or politician.

4. The day when everything changed was Tuesday, 9 October 2012. It wasn't the best of days to start with as it was the middle of school exams, though as a bookish girl I didn't mind them as much as my classmates.

   That morning we arrived in the narrow mud lane off Haji Baba Road in our usual procession of brightly painted rickshaws, sputtering diesel fumes, each one crammed with five or six girls. Since the time of the Taliban our school has had no sign and the ornamented brass door in a white wall … gives no hint of what lies beyond.

   For us girls that doorway was like a magical entrance to our own special world … Yet, outside the door to the school lay not only the noise and craziness of the city of Mingora … but also those like the Taliban who think girls should not go to school.

Reprinted by kind permission, 'I am Malala. The girl who stood up for Education and was shot by the Taliban' by Malala Yousafzai with Christina Lambs and the Orion Publishing Group.

5. … when our bus was called we ran down the steps. The other girls all covered their heads before emerging from the door … I was sitting on the left between Moniba and another girl … I remember the bus turned right off the main road at the army checkpoint as always … I don't remember any more … In reality what happened was we suddenly stopped … a young bearded man in light-coloured clothes had stepped into the road and waved the van down. 'Is this the Kushal School bus?' he asked our driver … 'I need information about some children.'… As he was speaking another young man in white approached the back of the van. 'Look, it's one of the journalists coming to ask for an interview,' said Moniba. Since I'd started speaking at events … to campaign for girls' education and against those like the Taliban who want to hide us away, journalists often came, even foreigners, though not like this in the road.

6. The man was wearing a peaked hat and had a handkerchief over his nose and mouth …'Who is Malala?' he demanded. No one said anything, but several of the girls looked at me. I was the only girl with my face not covered. That's when he lifted up a black pistol … Some of the girls screamed. Moniba tells me I squeezed her hand. My friends say he fired three shots … The first went through my eye socket and out under my left shoulder … My friends later told me the gunman's hand was shaking as he fired.

Question 1 (10 marks)

(a) What is the time difference between England and Pakistan?

1 hour

3 hours

5 hours

(b) Name three conveniences that Malala finds in England which are not available in Pakistan.

1 _____

2 _____

3 _____

(c) When Malala closes her eyes and imagines her valley, what does she see?

_____

_____

_____

_____

_____

(d) For what did Malala receive an award?

_____

_____

_____

(e) Who was Malala's rival in class?

_____

_____

(f) Who was Malala's best friend?

_____

_____

(g) What three things does Malala mention she shared with her best friend?

1 _____

2 _____

3 _____

(h) What career did Malala hope to pursue?

_____

_____

(i) What simile does Malala use to describe the door of her school?

_____

_____

_____

(j) What was the name of the school which Malala attended?

_____

_____

Question 2   (10 marks)

Identify three facts about Malala's life from your reading of the text.

1 _____

_____

2 _____

_____

3 _____

_____

Question 3

(10 marks)

Suggest three words to describe Malala's character and personality based on your reading of the extract.

1 _____

2 _____

3 _____

Question 4

(10 marks)

Based on the evidence of the text how do the lives of girls in Ireland differ from the lives of girls in Malala's community in Pakistan?

_____

_____

_____

_____

_____

_____

_____

_____

_____

_____

Question 5

(25 marks)

Give the title and author of a text that you studied on your course which dealt with the theme of education in an interesting and engaging way.

Title: _____

Author: _____

Write an account of what you found interesting about the treatment of education in your chosen text.

Optional Rough Work

Question 6

If you were to interview Malala on this text, what three questions would you ask her, to give you further insight into her life and the circumstances around her attack. Give your question and your reason for asking it.

Interview question 1:

_____

_____

_____

Reason for asking:

_____

_____

_____

_____

Interview question 2: _____

_____

_____

_____

Reason for asking: _____

_____

_____

_____

Interview question 3: _____

_____

_____

_____

Reason for asking: _____

_____

_____

_____

Section B   Responding Imaginatively – Poetry

Read this poem by Roger McGough and answer the questions which follow.

First Day At School

A millionbillionwillion miles from home
Waiting for the bell to go. (To go where?)
Why are they all so big, other children?
So noisy? So much at home they
Must have been born in uniform
Lived all their lives in playgrounds
Spent the years inventing games
That don't let me in. Games
That are rough, that swallow you up.

And the railings.
All around, the railings.
Are they to keep out wolves and monsters?
Things that carry off and eat children?
Things you don't take sweets from?
Perhaps they're to stop us getting out
Running away from the lessins. Lessin.
What does a lessin look like?
Sounds small and slimy.
They keep them in the glassrooms.
Whole rooms made out of glass. Imagine.

I wish I could remember my name
Mummy said it would come in useful.
Like wellies. When there's puddles.
Yellowwellies. I wish she was here.
I think my name is sewn on somewhere
Perhaps the teacher will read it for me.
Tea-cher. The one who makes the tea.

Question 7   **(15 marks)**

(a) Identify where, in the poem, the poet uses **exaggeration** and explain why, in your opinion,
    he uses it.

_____

_____

_____

_____

_____

_____

(b) Identify where, in the poem, the poet uses **personification** and explain why, in your opinion, he uses it.

_____

_____

_____

_____

_____

(c) Identify one **image** in the poem and describe its effect.

_____

_____

_____

_____

_____

Question 8   **(20 marks)**

Explain how the poet conveys (a) the confusion and (b) the insecurity of the child in the poem.

```
┌─────────────────────────────────────────────────┐
│                 Optional Rough Work               │
│                                                   │
│                                                   │
│                                                   │
│                                                   │
│                                                   │
│                                                   │
│                                                   │
│                                                   │
└─────────────────────────────────────────────────┘
```

_____

_____

_____

278

_____

_____

_____

_____

_____

_____

_____

_____

_____

_____

_____

_____

_____

_____

Question 9

(20 marks)

Write a description of your first day at school (real or imagined). Your description should capture the feelings and thoughts of a child. Your description may be written as a piece of prose or as a poem.

Optional Rough Work

_____

_____

_____

_____

_____

_____

_____

_____

_____

_____

_____

_____

_____

_____

_____

_____

_____

_____

Question 10

(20 marks)

Write five golden rules for parents to follow on their child's first day at school. The rules are intended to help the child and the parents cope with this new experience.

Optional Rough Work

Rule 1: _____

_____

_____

_____

Rule 2: _____

_____

_____

_____

_____

Rule 3: _____

_____

_____

_____

_____

Rule 4: _____

_____

_____

_____

_____

Rule 5: _____

_____

_____

_____

_____

Study the info-graphic on investment in the education of girls and answer the questions which follow.

BREAKING DOWN THE BARRIERS TO GIRLS' EDUCATION

Hindered by complex barriers ranging from social norms to geography, girls in developing countries remain more likely than boys to never learn how to read, write or do basic math. If we break down the barriers to quality education for all girls, we can unlock their potential and make important strides towards ending extreme poverty.

LEFT OUT AND LEFT BEHIND

63 MILLION girls were not in primary or lower-secondary school in 2013[1]

2X as many girls as boys will never start school[2]

There are approximately **781 MILLION** illiterate adults worldwide — 2/3 are women[3]

75% of girls enter primary school in Sub-Saharan Africa

SCHOOL — Only **8%** finish secondary school[4]

BENEFITS OF EDUCATING GIRLS

for themselves

for their families

for their communities & countries

1 additional school year → can increase a woman's earnings by **10%**

Girls with secondary schooling are **6x** less likely to marry as children compared to girls who have little or no education[5]

A child of a mother who can read is[7] **50% more likely** to live past age **5**

12.2 million children could avoid becoming stunted if their mothers had a secondary education[8]

+25% boost in agricultural output is possible by investing in girls' education in Sub-Saharan Africa[9]

+35% higher GDP per capita is associated with each additional year of education[10]

WHY AREN'T GIRLS IN SCHOOL?

TOP 10 BARRIERS TO GIRLS' EDUCATION

identified by Global Partnership for Education developing country partners (2012-2016)

1 SOCIAL AND CULTURAL FACTORS

2 EARLY MARRIAGE

38% OF SURVEYED COUNTRIES IDENTIFIED SOCIAL & CULTURAL FACTORS which can range from prioritizing a girl's role as wife and mother to not wanting girls to be taught by men, **as major barriers to girls' education**[11]

The earlier a girl gets married, the lower the probability that she attends secondary school[12]

COMPARED TO A GIRL WHO IS MARRIED AT 18:

A girl who gets married at **12** is **21** percentage points **less likely to attend secondary school**

A girl who gets married at **15** is **12** percentage points **less likely to attend secondary school**

When girls do more household chores than boys, such as fetching wood or water or caring for younger siblings, the cost of educating girls may seem higher to parents[13]

↓

40 BILLION HOURS spent by women in rural Africa fetching water each year[14]

3 **OPPORTUNITY COST OF SCHOOLING**

4 **LACK OF SEPARATE TOILETS FOR GIRLS & BOYS**

5 **LACK OF FEMALE TEACHERS**

6 **VIOLENCE AT SCHOOL OR ON THE WAY TO SCHOOL**

7 **DIRECT COST OF SCHOOLING**

8 **DISTANCE TO SCHOOL**

9 **LOW VALUE PLACED ON GIRLS' EDUCATION**

10 **POVERTY**

1 in 10 girls in Africa miss school during menstruation cycles [15] → **4 DAYS** x **12 TIMES A YEAR** = **20% OF ALL SCHOOL DAYS MISSED** [16]

28% In Yemen, 28% of cases where girls dropped out of school were decisions made by fathers due to the lack of female teachers [17]

10% In 40 low- and middle-income countries, up to 10% of adolescent girls aged 15–19 experienced forced sexual intercourse or other sexual acts in school [18]

In rural Benin [19]

Abolishing public primary school fees for all girls + Community mobilization =

1999 **64** girls for every 100 boys enrolled in primary school

2012 **89** girls for every 100 boys enrolled in primary school [20]

In Afghanistan, for every mile of extra travel needed to get to school [21]

ENROLLMENT DROPPED BY 19% GIRLS

ENROLLMENT ONLY FELL BY 1% BOYS

16 MILLION GIRLS will never start school compared to 8 million boys [22]

9X In sub-Saharan Africa, the poorest girls are 9x less likely to set foot in a classroom than the richest boys [23]

 GLOBAL PARTNERSHIP for EDUCATION

STRENGTHENING EDUCATION SYSTEMS DELIVERS RESULTS FOR GIRLS

The Global Partnership for Education (GPE) supports countries to develop, finance, and implement gender-responsive education sector plans

GPE partner developing countries have shown a a strong commitment to ensuring all girls are in school and learning, with promising results [24]

Training and recruiting female teachers

Increasing gender equality is a goal of GPE's 2016-2020 Strategy

Separate toilets for girls and boys

From 2000 to 2012 the **PERCENTAGE of GIRLS COMPLETING PRIMARY SCHOOL INCREASED** [24]

IN 2000 **54%** of girls completed primary school

IN 2013 **69%** of girls completed primary school

Gender-sensitive textbooks and teachers' guides

$ Disbursing 30% of grant funds only once a country demonstrates significant results in equity, efficiency, and learning outcomes

22% From 2000 to 2012 the number of **OUT-OF-SCHOOL GIRLS DROPPED BY 22%** [24]

 GLOBAL PARTNERSHIP for EDUCATION

The Global Partnership for Education supports 60+ developing countries to ensure that every child receives a quality basic education, prioritizing the poorest, most vulnerable and those living in fragile and conflict-affected countries.

Question 11 (10 marks)

(a) According to this info-graphic, how many girls were not in primary or secondary school in 2013?

_____

(b) According to this info-graphic, what percentage of girls finish secondary school in Sub-Saharan Africa?

_____

(c) According to this info-graphic, what is the number of adults in the world who cannot read or write?

_____

(d) According to this info-graphic, what three positive outcomes follow investment in girls' education?

1 _____

2 _____

3 _____

(e) Complete the sentence: "An additional year in school can increase a woman's earnings

by _____."

Question 12 (15 marks)

Based on the information contained in this info-graphic, write the script of a short talk to be delivered to your class. The title of your talk is: 'Why We Need to Invest in Girls' Education'.

284

Optional Rough Work

Additional Writing Space. Label all work clearly with the question number and part.

//:DON'T REPLY/
KEEP THE MESSAGE/
BLOCK THE SENDER/
TELL SOMEONE YOU TRUST://

WWW.WATCHYOURSPACE.IE

Edco EXAM PAPERS

The Complete Range for Junior Cycle

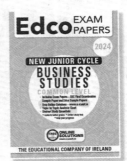

Edco EXAM PAPERS 2024 — NEW JUNIOR CYCLE BUSINESS STUDIES COMMON LEVEL — THE EDUCATIONAL COMPANY OF IRELAND

Edco EXAM PAPERS 2024 — NEW JUNIOR CYCLE ENGLISH HIGHER LEVEL — THE EDUCATIONAL COMPANY OF IRELAND

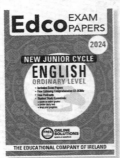

Edco EXAM PAPERS 2024 — NEW JUNIOR CYCLE ENGLISH ORDINARY LEVEL — THE EDUCATIONAL COMPANY OF IRELAND

Edco EXAM PAPERS 2024 — NEW JUNIOR CYCLE FRENCH COMMON LEVEL — THE EDUCATIONAL COMPANY OF IRELAND

Edco EXAM PAPERS 2024 — NEW JUNIOR CYCLE GAEILGE ARDLEIBHEAL — AN COMHLACHT OIDEACHAIS

Edco EXAM PAPERS 2024 — NEW JUNIOR CYCLE GAEILGE GNÁTHLEIBHEAL — AN COMHLACHT OIDEACHAIS

Edco EXAM PAPERS 2024 — NEW JUNIOR CYCLE GEOGRAPHY COMMON LEVEL — THE EDUCATIONAL COMPANY OF IRELAND

Edco EXAM PAPERS 2024 — NEW JUNIOR CYCLE GERMAN COMMON LEVEL — THE EDUCATIONAL COMPANY OF IRELAND

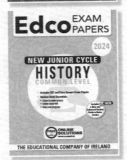

Edco EXAM PAPERS 2024 — NEW JUNIOR CYCLE HISTORY COMMON LEVEL — THE EDUCATIONAL COMPANY OF IRELAND

Edco EXAM PAPERS 2024 — NEW JUNIOR CYCLE HOME ECONOMICS COMMON LEVEL — THE EDUCATIONAL COMPANY OF IRELAND

Edco EXAM PAPERS 2024 — NEW JUNIOR CYCLE MATHEMATICS HIGHER LEVEL — THE EDUCATIONAL COMPANY OF IRELAND

Edco EXAM PAPERS 2024 — NEW JUNIOR CYCLE MATHEMATICS ORDINARY LEVEL — THE EDUCATIONAL COMPANY OF IRELAND

Edco EXAM PAPERS 2024 — NEW JUNIOR CYCLE MUSIC COMMON LEVEL — THE EDUCATIONAL COMPANY OF IRELAND

Edco EXAM PAPERS 2024 — NEW JUNIOR CYCLE RELIGIOUS EDUCATION COMMON LEVEL — THE EDUCATIONAL COMPANY OF IRELAND

Edco EXAM PAPERS 2024 — NEW JUNIOR CYCLE SCIENCE COMMON LEVEL — THE EDUCATIONAL COMPANY OF IRELAND

Edco EXAM PAPERS 2024 — NEW JUNIOR CYCLE SPANISH COMMON LEVEL — THE EDUCATIONAL COMPANY OF IRELAND

Edco EXAM PAPERS 2024 — NEW JUNIOR CYCLE WOOD TECHNOLOGY COMMON LEVEL — THE EDUCATIONAL COMPANY OF IRELAND

Exam Extras

> Updated Guide to Better Grades
> Exam Analysis Charts
> Study Planners and lots more...

edcoexampapers.ie

Ireland's No.1 Exam Papers

e-xamit
FREE ONLINE SOLUTIONS
Tutorials & Exam Advice
www.e-xamit.ie
*with selected papers

Available from your Local Bookshop
The Educational Company of Ireland

Edco — 2023/2024 School Year Planner

KEY DATES

Legend:
- ● Public Holidays
- ■ School Holidays
- ◆ Important Dates

2023/2024 School Year Planner

October 2023 mid-term break: All schools will close from Monday 30th October to Friday 3rd November 2023 inclusive.

Christmas 2023: All schools will close on Friday 22nd December 2023, which will be the final day of the school term. All schools will re-open on Monday 8th January 2024.

February 2024 mid-term break: Post-Primary schools will close from Monday 12th February to Friday 16th February 2024 inclusive.

Easter 2024: All schools will close on Friday 22nd March, which will be the final day of the school term. All schools will re-open on Monday 8th April 2024.

5th November – CAO application facility opens for 2024 applications

1st February – Normal closing date for CAO applications

1st May – Closing date for late CAO applications

1st July – Change Your Mind CAO Deadline

The start date for the Junior & Leaving Certificate Examinations 2024 will be Wednesday 7th June.

SEPTEMBER

1	Fri
2	Sat
3	Sun
4	Mon
5	Tues
6	Wed
7	Thurs
8	Fri
9	Sat
10	Sun
11	Mon
12	Tues
13	Wed
14	Thurs
15	Fri
16	Sat
17	Sun
18	Mon
19	Tues
20	Wed
21	Thurs
22	Fri
23	Sat
24	Sun
25	Mon
26	Tues
27	Wed
28	Thurs
29	Fri
30	Sat

OCTOBER

1	Sun
2	Mon
3	Tues
4	Wed
5	Thurs
6	Fri
7	Sat
8	Sun
9	Mon
10	Tues
11	Wed
12	Thurs
13	Fri
14	Sat
15	Sun
16	Mon
17	Tues
18	Wed
19	Thurs
20	Fri
21	Sat
22	Sun
23	Mon
24	Tues
25	Wed
26	Thurs
27	Fri
28	Sat
29	Sun
30	Mon ●
31	Tues

NOVEMBER

1	Wed ■
2	Thurs ■
3	Fri ■
4	Sat
5	Sun ◆
6	Mon
7	Tues
8	Wed
9	Thurs
10	Fri
11	Sat
12	Sun
13	Mon
14	Tues
15	Wed
16	Thurs
17	Fri
18	Sat
19	Sun
20	Mon
21	Tues
22	Wed
23	Thurs
24	Fri
25	Sat
26	Sun
27	Mon
28	Tues
29	Wed
30	Thurs

DECEMBER

1	Fri
2	Sat
3	Sun
4	Mon
5	Tues
6	Wed
7	Thurs
8	Fri
9	Sat
10	Sun
11	Mon
12	Tues
13	Wed
14	Thurs
15	Fri
16	Sat
17	Sun
18	Mon
19	Tues
20	Wed
21	Thurs
22	Fri
23	Sat
24	Sun
25	Mon ●
26	Tues ●
27	Wed ■
28	Thurs ■
29	Fri ■
30	Sat
31	Sun

JANUARY

1	Mon ●
2	Tues ■
3	Wed ■
4	Thurs ■
5	Fri ■
6	Sat
7	Sun
8	Mon
9	Tues
10	Wed
11	Thurs
12	Fri
13	Sat
14	Sun
15	Mon
16	Tues
17	Wed
18	Thurs
19	Fri
20	Sat
21	Sun
22	Mon
23	Tues
24	Wed
25	Thurs
26	Fri
27	Sat
28	Sun
29	Mon
30	Tues
31	Wed

FEBRUARY

1	Thurs ◆
2	Fri
3	Sat
4	Sun
5	Mon ●
6	Tues
7	Wed
8	Thurs
9	Fri
10	Sat
11	Sun
12	Mon ◆
13	Tues ◆
14	Wed ◆
15	Thurs ◆
16	Fri ◆
17	Sat
18	Sun
19	Mon
20	Tues
21	Wed
22	Thurs
23	Fri
24	Sat
25	Sun
26	Mon
27	Tues
28	Wed
29	Thurs

MARCH

1	Fri
2	Sat
3	Sun
4	Mon
5	Tues
6	Wed
7	Thurs
8	Fri
9	Sat
10	Sun
11	Mon
12	Tues
13	Wed
14	Thurs
15	Fri
16	Sat
17	Sun ●
18	Mon
19	Tues
20	Wed
21	Thurs
22	Fri
23	Sat
24	Sun
25	Mon ■
26	Tues ■
27	Wed ■
28	Thurs ■
29	Fri
30	Sat
31	Sun

APRIL

1	Mon ●
2	Tues ■
3	Wed ■
4	Thurs ■
5	Fri ■
6	Sat
7	Sun
8	Mon
9	Tues
10	Wed
11	Thurs
12	Fri
13	Sat
14	Sun
15	Mon
16	Tues
17	Wed
18	Thurs
19	Fri
20	Sat
21	Sun
22	Mon
23	Tues
24	Wed
25	Thurs
26	Fri
27	Sat
28	Sun
29	Mon
30	Tues

MAY

1	Wed ◆
2	Thurs
3	Fri
4	Sat
5	Sun
6	Mon ●
7	Tues
8	Wed
9	Thurs
10	Fri
11	Sat
12	Sun
13	Mon
14	Tues
15	Wed
16	Thurs
17	Fri
18	Sat
19	Sun
20	Mon
21	Tues
22	Wed
23	Thurs
24	Fri
25	Sat
26	Sun
27	Mon
28	Tues
29	Wed
30	Thurs
31	Fri

JUNE

1	Sat
2	Sun
3	Mon ●
4	Tues ◆
5	Wed ◆
6	Thurs
7	Fri
8	Sat
9	Sun
10	Mon
11	Tues
12	Wed
13	Thurs
14	Fri
15	Sat
16	Sun
17	Mon
18	Tues
19	Wed
20	Thurs
21	Fri
22	Sat
23	Sun
24	Mon
25	Tues
26	Wed
27	Thurs
28	Fri
29	Sat
30	Sun

JULY

1	Mon ◆
2	Tues
3	Wed
4	Thurs
5	Fri
6	Sat
7	Sun
8	Mon
9	Tues
10	Wed
11	Thurs
12	Fri
13	Sat
14	Sun
15	Mon
16	Tues
17	Wed
18	Thurs
19	Fri
20	Sat
21	Sun
22	Mon
23	Tues
24	Wed
25	Thurs
26	Fri
27	Sat
28	Sun
29	Mon
30	Tues
31	Wed

AUGUST

1	Thurs
2	Fri
3	Sat
4	Sun
5	Mon ●
6	Tues
7	Wed
8	Thurs
9	Fri
10	Sat
11	Sun
12	Mon
13	Tues
14	Wed
15	Thurs
16	Fri
17	Sat
18	Sun
19	Mon
20	Tues
21	Wed
22	Thurs
23	Fri
24	Sat
25	Sun
26	Mon
27	Tues
28	Wed
29	Thurs
30	Fri
31	Sat